OPENINGS AND CLOSINGS

Openings and Closings

DOROTHY STICKNEY

Doubleday & Company, Inc.
Garden City, New York
1979

Library of Congress Cataloging in Publication Data

Stickney, Dorothy.
Openings and closings.

Includes index.
1. Stickney, Dorothy.   2. Actors—United States—
Biography.   I. Title.
PN2287.S69A35   792'.028'0924[B]
ISBN 0-385-13222-0
Library of Congress Catalog Card Number 78–73195

TO HOWARD

Two with a light who match their steps and sing
Edna St. Vincent Millay

OPENINGS AND CLOSINGS

*A*LL THE WAY BACK TO TOWN IN THE CAR
I kept praying intermittently, "Please God, don't let them
have taken my heart-shaped ring—anything else I won't mind,
but please not that." The ring was a Victorian antique made of
chipped diamonds with a border of small rubies and a larger
ruby in the center of the heart. Howard had given it to me on
the stage in place of the prop ring we had always used at the
end of the second act. The occasion was the record-breaking
performance of *Life With Father.* It had had the longest run
of any play in Broadway history at that time. It had played
for seven years and was to play for nearly eight. Howard and
I had been Father and Mother, the red-haired Clare and Vinnie Day, for the first five years of its run at the beautiful old
Empire Theatre. Now we had come back to resume our parts
for this historic night.

I loved that ring because it was beautiful, because it was
somehow the summing up of all those *Life With Father* years,
and because Howard had given it to me. But beyond all that, I
loved it because it had become my talisman, my good-luck
charm—what I wore when I was scared or sad or uncertain, or

when there was a challenge to be met. Of course, since Howard's death, six years before, the ring had become even more necessary to me.

This weekend six of us had gone to the farm for an old-fashioned country Thanksgiving, and we had had it to perfection with the turkey, the cranberry sauce, the mince pie, the laughter and the warmth of long-time friendships, as well as the warmth from the huge fireplace. (Howard used to say it was big enough to lead a double life in.) Our party consisted of three writers, one literary agent, one publisher, and one actress—me.

The next day in the middle of a hilarious lunch the phone rang. It was darling, indispensable, irreplaceable Peggy, who had been secretary for Howard and me for so many years, and who had stayed on after Howard's death to help me cope. She was calling me from New York. Her shaky voice said, "Your house has been robbed."

She had gone to the house to pick up the mail and on her way up to the library had happened to glance through the dining-room door. The sideboard drawers were thrown on the floor—empty—all the silver was gone—the room was a shambles.

Having much better judgment than I would have had under the circumstances, she went no further but rushed outdoors. It isn't true that you can never find a policeman when you need one. Peggy did. Then she phoned me.

Robert Walston and I drove to New York, leaving the rest of the guests to clean up the remains of Thanksgiving. By the time we got here the police had finished exploring the house. They told me that nothing must be touched until the fingerprint men and the insurance people had checked. Peggy had already sent for a locksmith. I looked neither right nor left, but streaked up to my bedroom on the third floor. The ring was gone. So was everything else. Everything. Not even one piece of junk jewelry left. On the grass-green carpet was a litter of small cardboard boxes and velvet jewel cases. All empty. Obviously the thieves had planned to sort it out later at their leisure. There was hardly a place to step. My new fur coat, so recently delivered that the tags were still on it, was gone. The big box with my mother's wedding dress, and the small one (a shoe box, in fact) with mine had been pulled off a shelf. The Emerson and the Bible and the red hot-water bottle—my standbys in time of trouble—lay oddly in a heap together, under the bed table.

I stood there ankle deep in litter and unable to move. I was remembering vividly the time when Howard had given me that ring. It was the happiest night of my life—June 12, 1947. The audience who had seen the original performance in 1939 —all who could be located—were invited back for this special night. There were flowers and presents and programs printed on gold satin and tickets printed on gold cardboard. Jack Devereaux, the nephew of John Drew, who had played Clarence was back with us again, having enlisted, fought a war, and returned covered with decorations. Ruth Hammond, Dorothy Bernard, A. H. Van Buren, and Richard Sterling had never left the company at all. It was lovely, lovely, lovely! And loveliest of all, of course, was the ring—my surprise. The dialogue near the end of the second act went something like this:

CLARE: I was passing Tiffany's today and I picked up a little something for you. Thought you might like it.

He gives her the ring, which had, of course, always before been a prop ring from some costume jewelry counter, but this night it was real. I opened the little velvet box, put on this lovely piece of jewelry shaped like a heart, and almost went up in my lines. I managed to gasp in Vinnie's words, "Oh, Clare, what a beautiful ring! I don't know how to thank you." (I kissed Howard even longer and harder than the script called for.)

CLARE: Glad if it pleases you. (*He settles on the sofa with his newspaper.*)

VINNIE: Clare, this is the loveliest ring you ever bought me. Now that I have this you needn't buy me any more rings.

CLARE: Well, if you don't want any more—

VINNIE (*snuggling beside him on the sofa*): What I'd really like now is a nice diamond necklace.

CLARE (*shouts*): Vinnie! Do you know how much a diamond necklace costs?

VINNIE: I know, Clare. But don't you see this ring proves that I mean a little something to you. Now a nice diamond necklace—

CLARE (*roars*): Good God! If you don't know by this time how I feel about you—we've been married for twenty years and I've loved you every minute of it.

VINNIE (*incredulously*): What did you say, Clare?

CLARE: I said we've been married twenty years and I've loved you every minute of it, but if I have to buy out a jewelry store to prove it—

(VINNIE *starts to cry*. CLARE *looks at her in bewilderment*.)

CLARE: What have I done now?

VINNIE: It's all right—I am just so happy. You said you loved me. And this beautiful ring—that's something else I didn't expect. Oh, Clare—I love surprises.

The ring was a surprise to Vinnie, to say nothing of what a surprise and delight it was to me. A few more lines . . . and the scene curtain came down to warm laughter. The audience never suspecting they had been watching a play within a play.

Now—the curtain had come down on much more than a scene in a play. There was still an epilogue to be played out by me alone, and I'd better get at it. In a crisis I can cope. Let good times come, let everything happen as it should, let the sun shine, and let all be well with my world and I can fall apart, as you will see later on. But in emergencies I'm dandy—I function. Like the two occasions when the house was set afire—once by a cook who smoked reefers and once by a cook who burned voodoo candles in her room at night. Both times I had done the necessary things, and when the firemen arrived nothing was left of the fire but a house full of smoke.

I left my room and didn't return to it until I went to bed that night. The next room was one where I had been working on the scrapbooks—a forty-year record of the stage. The books had been promised to the New York Theatre Library. I was years behind and I had been trying to catch up and get them in order. They were shoved to the floor and scattered so that the big table-top desk could be more thoroughly ransacked. In the closet of that room was the only thing in the whole house that had ever been kept locked—a metal strongbox containing some letters, some valentines, silly verses we had written each other, our wills, the deed to the farmhouse, etc. They had smashed it open and found, thank God, there wasn't a thing in it that they wanted.

On the second floor little time had been wasted on Howard's bedroom as the drawers and closets are empty now. And in the library, across the hall, where Howard Lindsay and Russel Crouse had written so many plays, and where a lot of theatre memorabilia was kept on shelves, all they found of value was some petty cash and a roll of stamps.

Downstairs the dining room needed only a confirming glance, but I was scared to open the opposite door and find out what had happened in the living room. I am an incurable collector and that is where the music boxes and the fairy lights live. My treasured fairy lights, those early Victorian confections consisting of a small glass saucer to hold the candle and a colored glass chimney over it shaped like a rose, a dome, a lighthouse, a birdcage, all sorts of fantasies. They were described in an advertisement of that long-ago period as being "appropriate for use in conservatories or ballrooms." The fairy lights were intact, standing on their glass shelves in the bay window with the sunlight shining through their lovely colors. The music boxes had been opened but left unharmed. My thieves were proper thieves, not vandals, and I was grateful.

However, there was also in the living room a handsome old chest which once stood on the stage in *State of the Union*, the play that had won the Pulitzer Prize for Lindsay and Crouse. In it I kept memories of my family. The Stickneys have always been great savers and "put-er away-ers." There were records of my grandparents, letters written one hundred years ago, souvenirs of Father, Mother, diaries, old North Dakota newspapers, telegrams, poems—mine and other people's—

pamphlets, and the copies of some office files and love letters of a young doctor in Dakota Territory to a young dressmaker in Vermont—Victor Hugo Stickney to Maggie Hayes. They turned out to be my father and mother. Also, dozens of pictures—some of them are pictures of me that range from a towheaded two-year-old wearing big black glasses to a frightened-looking ingenue just arrived in New York, to a recent photograph of a grande dame onstage belting out a song with five chorus boys behind her in a rock musical called *Pippin*. The contents of the drawers had been scattered everywhere. The living room was deep in personal history.

I could hear noises from the hall where men were boarding up the small glass doorpane which my visitors had so neatly cut with their burglar tools. I began to realize for the first time what those ominous words "breaking and entering" really meant. Every drawer, every closet invaded by persons unknown. That may be the worst thing about a burglary—the invasion of one's personal world. The experience was an ugly shock. I knew I would not cry because not to cry was the first thing I had ever had to learn. I learned it at a very early age, and the habit had persisted through the years. However, I did promise myself a nice nervous breakdown as soon as all the police had gone, the insurance men had asked their last question, and the burglar alarm had been installed. But even that had to be postponed because I had made a commitment to do a benefit performance, within a few days, of my one-woman show about Edna St. Vincent Millay; and the upset at home meant that I had to concentrate even harder than usual on the job at hand. So, the house must remain a wreck for the time being, as I was the only one who could sort it out and put it together again.

I've gone into detail of this all too common occurrence for a reason. The reason is coincidence. Coincidence should be used sparingly in the theatre because it is such a convenient device that it seldom convinces an audience. Coincidence, however, in real life is a fact. Certainly it has been in mine. With me that long arm has been so very, very long that it would make bad playwriting.

The publisher, who was one of our Thanksgiving party on the farm, had suggested a year or so before that I write a book, a biography. I thought we had both forgotten about it, so I was surprised, flattered, and incredulous when he brought it up again and persisted with the idea. Even being willing to buy it sight unseen. I've been writing all my life—putting things down—diaries, letters, verses, speeches, pieces about my dad and mother, but all of this had been fragmentary and, for the most part, private. A book—that was quite a different thing. What would I write about?

On midnight forays to the kitchen for a snack or to pet the cats, I would sometimes stop in the doorway of one of the rooms and look in.

I don't know exactly when it occurred to me that my thieves might have done me a service. There was my life, and all that touched it, scattered on the floors of the house. What they had left was of no value to them. What was of value to me? What was really of value? I had better pick up the pieces and find out. Perhaps here was the book.

From the top of the litter I picked up my father's cattle brand—a yellowed leaflet on which was a picture of a steer with a mark like a triangular flag on its flank, and underneath the name V. H. Stickney, Chicago Stock Registry.

Dad once told me that when he came to Dakota Territory, in the 1880s, the town of Dickinson consisted of six saloons and a post office. Young Victor Hugo Stickney had just acquired his degree in medicine from Dartmouth. It didn't take as long to become a doctor then as it does now. He had worked his way through the college years by shoveling coal and waiting table in the winters, and in summers doing any work he could get—helping road builders and assisting in a mental hospital. Incidentally, because he had studied geology, he was once hired by a scientist who had been a patient in that hospital to take a job on a sailing ship headed for the Cape Verde Islands to search for guano deposits.

That voyage must have been something straight out of Robert Louis Stevenson, but you would never have guessed it from Father's laconic diary. He was meticulous about recording latitude and longitude and weather, but he gave short shrift to a mutiny aboard, a hurricane, and of being becalmed for two weeks in the Sargasso sea and living on chocolate and water until they could make the next port for food supplies. Father never touched chocolate the rest of his life. I had to learn of this adventure years later. One entry in his diary says simply, "Shot a whale"—nothing more that day.

Victor Stickney and Maggie Hayes grew up on adjoining farms near Tyson, Vermont, until he went to Dartmouth to learn to be a doctor and she went to the nearby town of Ludlow to be a dressmaker. There were ten Stickney children and eight Hayes children. Maggie was second-generation Irish. Her parents had come over from Kerry and Cork, and like all the Irish, of course, were "descended from the kings."

Victor's kin were Yankees as far back as there was any such thing. His forebears had left England to come to the New World in 1638—William and Elizabeth—and had made their home in the village of Rowley, Massachusetts, not many miles from a settlement called Boston, where there had recently been built a church. My father's grandparents had found their way to Vermont. In clearing that stony land for farming they had helped to build miles of beautiful stone fences—a joy to the eyes of generations to come, surely less than a joy to the hardy farmers who did the clearing. I have been told that my grandfather obtained a law degree through a correspondence course from Harvard. Could this be true? Maybe. At least I know that it *is* true he ran the village post office and was a farmer besides.

I never knew any of my grandparents and had not the slightest curiosity about them until it was too late to ask. However, I got a pretty clear picture of the Stickney ones, thanks to an inscription on a tombstone. One summer when Howard and I took a holiday in Vermont, we spent a lovely afternoon exploring the fragrant back-country roads and came upon a small forgotten cemetery. Years of neglect showed in the wild grass that covered it waist high, almost obliterating the weather-worn granite slabs that were the headstones. But there was one monument in white marble that stood higher than the others. The inscription read "John Winslow Stickney —born 1818—died 1899—A completely honest man." And below it, "Ann Pinney Stickney, wife of John Winslow Stickney—born 1831—died 1904—The law of kindness was on her tongue." We laughed, and decided that if he was a completely honest man, and in Vermont that meant *completely,* what a fortunate thing for both of them and for their children that "The law of kindness was on her tongue."

A lifetime later there came an echo of that golden afternoon to comfort me when I was in desperate need. It was the first bleak Christmas after Howard's death and I was alone in the house trying to wrap presents. I had run out of cards to go on the packages and was looking through a box of unused cards from Christmases past. Among them I found a small folder. It was bright red with holly and sparkles and had been attached with a little red cord to some present that Howard had once given me. Inside, in Howard's handwriting, it said: "To my wife—the law of kindness is on her tongue, from her completely honest husband."

The Stickneys didn't bother much with their two daughters' names. They were just Elizabeth and Frances. But the eight sons were all given grand resounding names to live up to. There was John Thatcher, Joseph Horatio, William Wallace, Victor Hugo, Rollin Winslow, Henry Elmer, Edgar Russell, and Highland Orlando. William Wallace, the only one the family had been able to help through college, grew up to be the rock-ribbed Republican governor of Vermont who seconded Coolidge's nomination for the presidency with three sparse paragraphs. One paragraph I particularly cherish for its Vermontness. My uncle Will says of his friend Calvin Coolidge: "For a lifetime I have known the President's father intimately, and well recollect his grandfather. In truth it can be stated as family characteristics, which the President exemplifies to a marked degree, that they never wasted any time, they never wasted any words, and they never wasted any public money."

Only two of the ten Stickney children ever went farther

afield than Boston. The two were Highland Orlando, who coached football at Yale, became a professional polo player, and died young of an athlete's heart. The other was Victor Hugo who went to Dakota Territory to be a doctor.

Before he left, he and Maggie Hayes were engaged, and she would journey west to marry him as soon as he could earn enough money to support them and as soon as he could get a house for them to live in. That took two years. In the small room that was her dressmaker shop in Ludlow, Maggie had the time, the love, and the dressmaker's skill to create her beautiful trousseau, and to dream her dreams about what it would be like for a girl who had never been on a train overnight to set out for a place called Dakota Territory to a town called Dickinson where her Victor would be waiting to marry her.

The town of Dickinson was actually something more than the six saloons and a post office of my dad's first impression. It was a town made all too familiar to us on the television and movie screen. A huddle of false-front buildings, set down in the middle of a vast and empty prairie, where the sky was enormous and overpowering, and where the wind blew relentlessly. There were then only about six hundred inhabitants, but the town, surprisingly, had a newspaper, the Dickinson *Press*, and a photographer, Mr. Osborn. Thanks to them, I know more about the Dakota Territory of my parents' first years there than I could possibly have learned otherwise. Mr. Osborn had started taking pictures some years before my father's time. Photographs of buffalo hides, piles six feet high in the road, waiting for shipment east, of stock-loading pens near the brand-new Northern Pacific Railroad tracks, of Jerry Hayes's blacksmith shop, of roundups and cattle brandings, of bands of Sioux and Gros Ventres in full regalia camped just outside of town at the season of the big hunt. And many years later, pictures of my sister and me in our lace bonnets and starched white dresses.

The old letters, Father's office files, the diaries, the photographs, and the newspaper have made the time and place so vivid that I catch myself actually believing I was there.

The Dickinson *Press* supplied all the Slope country with local news. I have inherited four years' worth of random items from its pages: "Shooting in the streets at night is to be discouraged." "Vic Smith, champion shot of Dakota, brought in two buffalo calves and a cow from the range. He thinks they can be raised and domesticated. He believes this plan is the only way to save the buffalo from being entirely exterminated." "The Northern Pacific Railroad is now finished to within seventy miles of Helena, Montana." "Dr. Victor H. Stickney arrived last Saturday from Tyson, Vermont, and has located here for the practice of medicine. He is a graduate of Dartmouth College and comes highly recommended as a good physician. He may be found at Davis and Fowler's Drugstore." "About 700 Indians—Crees, Gros Ventres and Mandans in town from Fort Berthold. Eight hundred ponies, ninety wagons. When coming over the hill north of town it reminded one of a vast army and made the hair of the tenderfoot stand on end. This is the season of the year when they go on the Grand Hunt and ceremony. Now bound for the southern buffalo range about fifty miles distant. They are camping one mile south of town on the banks of the Hart River." "The Villard House had a grand opening ball the week of August 16th. Ice cream, cake and oranges were served. Mr. and Mrs. Lomereaux furnished excellent music for dancing until the wee small hours."

Here is part of the first letter my father sent from Dakota Territory to his father in Vermont—a tenderfoot's description of the western country that was to be his home.

My Dear Father,
    Your welcome letter arrived and I can tell you I was glad to get it.

Then:

This is flat country and dotted with small hills called "buttes," which stick up here and there on the prairie. There is one called Chalk Butte where they get material they use for plastering houses. All they do is mix it with hair and water and it stands anything but water as well as lime and sand would. Last night the rain came through the roof over my bed and softened the plastering so you could stick your finger into it. There are no trees here within forty or fifty miles. The soil grows buffalo grass in abundance. It cures on the root and the ponies and cattle keep fat on it all winter. The principal business here is hunting and herding cattle. They graze all the way from Mexico and some of the herds number thirty thousand head. They are looked after by the inveterate cowboy. The cowboy is noted as being the best revolver shot, the finest horseman, the most enthusiastic swearer, and the worst man in a row that America produces. His appearance is unique. All that is essential for his existence is a revolver. Don't make any mistake here—in a cowboy's mind a revolver weighs nothing under five pounds and carries forty-two cartridges with fifty grains of powder. Give him a pair of leather britches (called chaps), high-heeled boots, a set of jingling spurs, a red shirt, a sombrero (Mexican hat) and he's fixed. But to see him actually in his glory give him ten bits ($2.50) to get drunk on and now look out. He's ready to fight, shoot, run his horse, or swear for money, fun or because he's actually mad. And if he's mad, don't question his veracity. The other day a tenderfoot (provincial for inexperienced)— my father explains to his father—called him a liar and was filled so full of lead that it was a question whether to bury the body or send it to the Bismarck bullet factory.

But the cowboy has sterling Christian qualities too. He never banters on a trade, and if you do him a favor he'll remember it forever. They stick together and if you injure one it's the fight of the whole pack.

The hunters, as a rule, are quiet, peaceable men in town, but on the range they don't make any more bones about sending a Red Man to the Happy Hunting Grounds than they do of killing a buffalo. The Indians steal hides and ponies from them, and within the last fortnight they have burned the prairie completely over between the two

Cannonball Rivers (see map), and the buffalo are all gone. The Sioux are the ones that did the mischief, and the country upholds, or at least allows, this. Many think there is trouble brewing among the Indians. Three tribes have camped here since I came.

Wild game is abundant—and you can get buffalo, deer, bear, antelope, wild sheep, civits, wolves, geese, ducks and prairie chickens. Sometimes deer and antelope can be seen from town. I shot four ducks at one shot the other day, and you know I am no brag of a shot. A great deal of wild meat is shipped East from here. Thirty miles west in the Bad Lands the geological formation is fantastic. I have seen a petrified tree stump that you could count the rings on as easily as you could that of an ash at home.

I am in good health and enjoying myself. I don't get much practice but the little I do get pays, and I shall make something more than a living this winter. We have plenty of snow, and it is very cold, but one can stand a lot of cold here. How is Mother getting on? My food basket for the train held out first rate, and I often think of the dear hands that put it up. Please send me a Vermont paper once in a while, and I wish you would nail up that box of books and send it along.

Hoping to hear from you, I am

Your dutiful son,
Victor

It touches my heart to read this, his first letter home, dated 1884, and in the same envelope to find a newspaper dated 1957 with the headline DR. V. H. STICKNEY ELECTED TO THE NATIONAL COWBOY HALL OF FAME IN OKLAHOMA CITY. My father was voted one of its first ten members, and is in the company of such men as Theodore Roosevelt, Will Rogers, and Gary Cooper.

I wish Dad could have known that his towheaded daughter would one day be represented in a neighboring Hall of Fame —this one known as "The Teddy Roosevelt Rough Riders" in the capitol building in Bismarck, North Dakota. I am designated an honorary "Colonel." How Dad would have smiled at that! I am there along with Eric Sevareid, Peggy Lee, General Harold K. Johnson, Lawrence Welk, Roger Maris, and others of a widely scattered group, all born and raised in small towns in North Dakota. I wonder if they had listened to train whistles in the night as I had when I was a child? I wonder if the whistles had spoken to them of faraway places?

Historians of Dakota Territory write of my father as "The Cowboy Doctor." He had become so much part of that prairie country. It had become so completely his home that it is hard to remember that he ever belonged to Vermont. He never wore chaps nor a red shirt nor high-heeled boots nor a revolver, but he made his calls on horseback or in a sleigh or in a buckboard to visit the sick or injured in the bleak and lonely obscurity of a ranch house or a cow camp, and if he got there too late he often stayed on to help dig the grave or to read the burial service. He was as much at home on horseback as any cowpuncher on the range.

Here is a description of my father in the words of Hermann Hagedorn from his book called *Roosevelt in the Bad Lands*.

Dr. Stickney was the only physician within 150 miles in any direction. He was a quiet, lean man with a warm smile and friendly eyes, a sense of humor and a zest for life. He had a reputation for never refusing a call whatever the distance or the weather. Sometimes he rode with a guide. More often, he rode alone. He knew the landmarks for a hundred miles in any direction. At night, when the trail grew faint, he held his course by the stars. When an unexpected blizzard swept down upon him and the snow hid the trail, he sought a brush patch in a coulee and tramped back and forth to keep himself from freezing, until the storm had spent itself. It was a life of extraordinary devotion. Stickney took it with a laugh, blushing when men spoke well of him, and called it the day's work. If you were totally incapacitated, you sent word to his office in Dickinson. The stretch of country he covered was not quite as large as New England but almost. And he covered it on horseback, in a buckboard; in the cab of a wildcat engine or a caboose of a freight train on occasion, or a handcar. He was utterly fearless and, it seemed, utterly tireless. At grueling speed he rode until his horse stood with heaving sides and nose drooping, then, at some ranch, he changed to another horse and rode on. Over a hundred miles or more he would ride relays at a speed that seemed incredible, and at the end of the journey, operate with a calm hand for a gunshot wound or a cruelly broken bone, sometimes on the box of a mess wagon turned upside down on the prairie.

My sister and I came late in our parents' marriage. By the time we arrived it was no longer Dakota Territory but had become the state of North Dakota.

When I knew my mother she was beautiful—at least I thought she was. Perhaps she wasn't. Perhaps it was just that I loved her so much. Mother had grown plump through the years. She had black, black hair, olive skin, bright blue eyes, and very white teeth—and even when she wasn't smiling her mouth and eyes looked as if she was just about to. As a young woman, as a bride, she was really lovely. The old photographs prove that. She was tiny then. I know because when I was twelve years old I found her wedding dress. It was a rainy day, and I was rummaging through the big chest in the attic, trying to find clothes to "play show" in.

The chest was full of such things as the baby dresses and shoes of my sister and me, discarded rag dolls, odds and ends of things that had gone out of fashion; my father's Masonic sword and the big American flag that was hung from a window on Decoration Day and the Fourth of July.

At the very bottom of the chest was Mother's wedding dress, packed safely away (she thought), wrapped in tissue and tied up in a big cardboard box. A lovely dress of cream-colored satin brocade, trimmed with soft cream-colored lace, and it even had lace and hand hemstitching on the inside where it didn't show. Its pointed bodice was stiffly boned and its waist measured eighteen inches. Of course I put it on and it fitted my twelve-year-old frame perfectly except for the length and some hooks that wouldn't fasten around my middle. It looked brand-new, as if it had never been worn, and indeed it never had been, but I didn't learn that story until years later.

The dad that I remember had sandy hair that must have been blond, like mine, when he was a child. He had many outside interests. He had managed to accumulate a fine library. He read much. He worked hard, and of necessity was away from home frequently. Sometimes his call on the sick in remote parts of the country would keep him from home for days at a time. Unlike Mother, he had the reticence inherited from his Yankee ancestors, so I never got to know him well until I grew up, nor did I appreciate how very special he was. I envied my older sister because she looked exactly like Mother while I looked like Dad.

Mother was warm, ebullient, gay, loving, and outgoing—and always there—always available in both good times and bad. She was vocationally a mother just as my father was vocationally a doctor. I adored her with such blind devotion that even now—even at this distance—it is hard for me to see her as a person, as anything other than my beloved mother. Both my parents in their different ways brought something of Vermont with them to Dakota Territory.

Dickinson *Press* items: "Stark County organized with Dickinson as the county seat." "Dr. Victor H. Stickney, who came here a short time ago from Tyson, Vermont, was appointed County Physician and Surgeon by the Board of Commissioners at their session last Monday." This is not surprising as he must surely have been the only doctor in the county. "Fifteen cars of lumber arrived this week. Wood and decar pails, washtubs, washboards, baskets, brooms, and all kind of wood ware at the Dickinson Hardware Company." Wood was a precious commodity in that treeless country. Some shrubs and a few cottonwood trees grew along the banks of the Hart River, but that was all. "President Villard, of the Northern Pacific, announces the golden spike to be driven with the silver mallet only 18 miles from Helena, Montana." "You can find Briars

Whiskey and also Hennessey brands at Eade's." "Forty below zero yesterday." "Dr. V. H. Stickney has received twenty volumes of standard medical works as a Christmas present from his brother, W. W. Stickney, who is clerk of the Vermont House of Representatives. They are worth about $60 and are a fine and useful present." "Good sleighing." "Daughters of the Prairie giving oyster supper." "Nine human skulls and other bones, pieces of a compass, and a spoon found by George Rand twelve miles north of town. Could this be the party that started from St. Paul in '67, seeking a more direct route to the Montana gold mines, and were never heard of again?" "Dr. Stickney can be found in his new office in the Lawrence Building upstairs." "Mrs. Vic Smith, coming home on horseback, was lost on the prairie from Saturday evening until Monday. Hunting parties were out looking for her." "Dr. Stickney was taken very sick with spinal meningitis and for two days his life was despaired of. Oh, but his many friends are pleased to see him on the streets again."

The newspaper item is all I ever knew of this. Who took care of him? His living quarters must have been, of course, that new office upstairs in the Lawrence Building. There was no other doctor within a hundred miles in any direction. Of course no nurse. Maggie Hayes would not arrive until a year later. How did he survive? His own natural strength and the help of good neighbors must have pulled him through. I wish I knew. I wish I could say "Thank you" across time and space to someone.

"Costello's Circus showed here in June." "There is talk of putting down board sidewalks in town." "Beginning April first trains will leave St. Paul for Dickinson daily." "Dr. V. H. Stickney has purchased the Gibbon's Building" (it was originally the post office) "and two lots on the corner of Sims and Main Streets. This is valuable property to own. He is improving the building by raising the upper story two feet, thus making the ceilings higher." This is the house where my parents lived out their lives and where my sister and I were born and grew up.

"Sioux on thieving raid stole ponies and hides from white

hunters. Set fire to grass so buffalo would go onto their reservation. Even burned cattle range. High feeling."

"While crossing the river at Gladstone on Tuesday, the buggy was turned over by the high water and Dr. Stickney took an icy bath in the raging Hart River." "Population of Dickinson is now 750." "Welches Comedy Company gave one of their side-splitting entertainments in Collester Hall. Original hits and mimicry of James Welch." "Dickinson Literary and Debating Society organized."

"Dr. V. H. Stickney and his bride, who were married at the Inter-Ocean Hotel in Mandan, arrived here on the Northern Pacific. The happy couple received congratulations from a host of friends."

When Maggie Hayes left home, her beautiful wedding dress and the rest of her trousseau must have been carefully sacheted and packed in a big new trunk. No doubt she wore a dark-colored, practical little traveling dress of her own making for the long, long trip. She probably had something fresh for getting spruced up in when she arrived in Dickinson to be met by her fiance, who would have all the wedding arrangements made. I wonder what that journey with several changes of trains in strange cities was like for a young girl who had never been out of Vermont? She must have been pretty worn-out and travel-stained by the time the train reached Mandan.

And it was at Mandan, one hundred miles east of Dickinson, that Victor surprised her by boarding the train. His greeting was "Get off the train, Maggie. We have to get married here because this is where the priest is. The train will wait twenty minutes." So they hurried across the road to the Inter-Ocean Hotel and were married, and Mother wore her dusty little traveling dress, and the train waited twenty minutes, and they journeyed another hundred miles west over the flat prairie to Dickinson, and to the "valuable property on Sims and Main Streets."

There is another costume from her trousseau which she did get a chance to wear at least once—at least long enough to have her picture taken to send back East to her family. The costume (and costume is the right word) was her New England version of a lady's riding habit. She is photographed against the open prairie. She is wearing a trailing wine-red velvet skirt, a rigidly boned little black bodice, jet buttoned up to her chin, a tiny stiff hat like a miniature derby, tight black gloves, and the corners of a white lace handkerchief show from a pocket near her shoulder. Next to her with drooping head stands a shamefaced Indian pony. The pony is wearing— a side saddle.

Father must have sent East for the side saddle. I doubt that Mother ever liked horses. I think she was afraid of them. I never saw her ride, but she must have been on a horse a few times because once she told me, "When I first came here, I used to think that I'd see something different every time I rode over the next rise of ground—but I never did."

I wonder if she missed the hills and trees and brooks and winding roads she left behind? Why, oh why, didn't I ask more questions?

She once told me that when she first came West she used to be frightened when an Indian or two stood looking in the kitchen window watching her while she worked at the stove. But she soon realized they were not interested in her scalp, only in what she was cooking. So she would beckon them in and they would squat on the kitchen floor until she gave them her hot doughnuts.

Here I go, actually believing I was there, actually smelling those hot doughnuts when I'm really in my bedroom in New York—picking up her beautiful wedding dress from where it lies half out of its box on my closet floor, as the burglars had left it. I rescued my own wedding dress from the broken shoe box and put it in with Mother's. Mine is a skimpy wisp of pink shantung of the nineteen twenties, the flapper era. It had been the best my stock wardrobe trunk could produce at the time. It hardly deserved to be in such elegant company, but I put them together, tied up the box, and stored them both away on the top shelf again.

One of my father's earliest patients was a young man from a ranch near Medora, a small town in the Bad Lands about thirty miles from Dickinson. The young man had met him on the street; he was limping and asked where he could find a doctor. Father told him that he was the only doctor. The man replied that he was a deputy sheriff and that he had just put two men in jail—and that his feet were in pretty bad shape and needed some attention. My father learned that two days before this young man had succeeded in tracking down two outlaws. They had stolen a boat on the Little Missouri River, a crime then considered as mean as horse stealing and almost as severely punishable. He had followed them downstream, spotted their campfire, taken them by surprise and arrested them as they were making camp for the night.

It was early spring. He had taken the pair on a two days' journey over the prairie, sometimes fording streams filled with floating ice. The two men rode in a buckboard and the deputy sheriff had walked behind them carrying a gun. He dared not sleep during the thirty-mile trek to Dickinson. It was only after he had landed them in jail that he inquired of the first man he met on the street where he could find a doctor. He said his name was Theodore Roosevelt.

My father wrote of their first meeting in these words: "He had breezed into town from the north in the early spring of 1886. A strange type of fellow in large spectacles and tattered garments. His face was sunburned, his feet bruised and blistered from a long tramp over rough trails. He was a sparse, energetic young man, very much alive and very much in earnest.

"He didn't seem unduly worn out or tired, though he had had no sleep for forty-eight hours. He was all teeth and eyes. He was thrilled by the adventure he had been through but didn't seem to think he'd done anything commendable. In his own phrase he was 'pleased as Punch' at having participated in a real adventure. When I went home I told my wife I had met the most peculiar and at the same time the most interesting man I had ever come to know. I could see that he was a man of brilliant ability, but I couldn't understand why he was out there on the frontier."

It was a personal tragedy that had first sent Roosevelt to the western country. A poignant grief had come into his life—his cherished wife and his beloved mother had died within twenty-four hours of each other. He was seeking peace of mind and a strenuous life among strangers to reinforce his physical strength and to regain his healthy outlook. He bought a ranch in the Bad Lands; one couldn't get much farther away or to a much stranger country than the Bad Lands of Dakota Territory.

———————

In the Slope country there were only two profitable businesses to invest in—game hunting and sheep or cattle raising. So my father registered a cattle brand and when he had saved a little money he bought a few head of cattle to be fattened up on the prairie grass and eventually shipped to the Chicago Stockyards. Perhaps someday he could make a profit. He did, and certainly in a way he never could have expected.

Here is a letter from my friend Arthur Parker of Dickinson. Arthur was considerably older than I, but his parents had been contemporaries of my parents. He was a loyal westerner and treasured all the stories that his father and mother loved to tell of the early days. It was my good luck that he shared them with me. This is the letter exactly as he wrote it.

Friend Dorothy: Herewith I send you a little story that you may not know. I can still remember my folks talking about it when they had visitors from Wibeaux, Montana.

Sidney Tarbell was a young cowboy who worked for Pierre Wibeaux on his ranch—the "Big W." Mr. and Mrs. Tarbell were good friends of my father and mother, who were especially fond of the Tarbells' son, Sidney. In fact, Sid Tarbell was very well liked by everyone. Pierre Wibeaux made him a foreman because he was a special favorite. When Pierre returned from his frequent trips to Europe he used to bring nice presents to Sid—hand-forged silver spurs from Belgium or beautiful custom-made beaver hats from Italy.

While branding calves on the North "W" one day, Sid's horse threw him and he broke a lot of bones—compound fractures—and way out there in Montana, eighty miles from the railroad and from Dickinson, Sid died.

Dr. Stickney made a valiant ride in an effort to reach Sidney in time. He made an 80-mile ride that I don't think has ever since been equaled in Dakota or Montana—a fresh horse, the best and fastest at every ranch he passed. When he got there it was too late. Sidney was dead.

Cowboys talked about it over campfires for many years after, and they decided that here was a young man they wanted to stay in the country. Now who it was that did it, no one ever knew or cared. But every once in a while, when they were branding calves on the roundup, and the boss wasn't breathing down their necks, someone would say, "Let's brand one for the Doctor." And a nice healthy calf would be turned loose with the doctor's brand on it.

Four years later a carload of fat 4-year-old steers came into the Chicago yards under Dr. Stickney's brand and, as usual, the check was forwarded to the man who registered the brand—and your father was in the cattle business.

I think these fellows figured out and practiced the first social security in North Dakota if not in the nation.

Hope you enjoyed your visit in Dickinson. Come again soon,

> Yours truly,
> Arthur Parker

I sat down on the flowered red carpet in the living room and picked up a welter of baby pictures to be sorted out and put back in the top drawer where they came from. My mother was an amateur photographer. She had a big box camera. She loved taking pictures of her children in all stages of dress and undress. And then, of course, there were the professional pictures taken by Mr. Osborn—the same Mr. Osborn who had photographed the Wild West years before we were born. But this was only when our straight hair (done up in curl rags the night before) was sufficiently curled and we were sufficiently starched for the occasion.

Something else to be put back in the top drawer was a battered ledger with copies of typewritten letters covering two years of my father's life, which also happened to be the first two years of my life.

He always used a typewriter and carbon paper, a habit which I have inherited. It was a way of keeping his office files, but the letters spilled over into other things—letters to my mother when she had me in the hospital in St. Paul, letters to relatives explaining why he could not make the trip East for his parents' golden-wedding celebration, and desperate letters to St. Paul specialists trying to find out what was the matter with his youngest child's eyes. Of course I had to pore over the ledger again, and, as always, with a lump in my throat.

Victor and Maggie had waited a long time for their two children. Finally my older sister came long. She was pretty and healthy and a thoroughly satisfactory baby, who had the misfortune of being born on Christmas Eve. When I came along I was none of those things, but I did have the good fortune of being born on Midsummer Day. (Obviously better for birthday parties and presents.) They named her Marjorie Ann. And I can remember a nonsense rhyme being chanted with laughter in the voices:

> "Marjorie Ann Belinda Lou
> Has fallen in love with a timbucktoo
> His eyes are green and his hair is blue.
> Oh dear! Oh dear! What's she coming to?"

I was a twin. My twin was born dead. That's all I was ever told about it. I don't even know whether it was a boy or a girl. From the first there was something very wrong with my eyes. No one ever seemed to know exactly what caused it. Could it have been something as specific as a bad infection? Those were the days before penicillin and the sulfa drugs, and if an eye infection could not be cured people simply lost their sight.

Here are some bits and pieces culled at random from my father's ledger. This was written in January to the doctor who was treating my eyes at a hospital in St. Paul.

"Dear Dr. McDevit: Mrs. Stickney and the baby have just returned home from St. Paul. Dorothy is much improved and I am in hopes she will have no more trouble. I will carry out your instructions for treatment. Thank you for all your kindness to my wife and family."

*　　*　　*

(In February he wrote:)
"Dear Doctor: The baby's eyes have suddenly become worse again. She can not stand light at all. Yesterday we could not induce her to open her eyes until evening. Today she has them opened in a darkened room at noon. Her condition causes me alarm, and I think she will require to be under treatment again for some time. Mrs. Stickney and I will bring the baby to St. Paul as soon as possible."

(I was taken to St. Paul. It was nearly eight months before Mother brought me home again. In the meanwhile, bills had to be collected, calls had to be made, and six-year-old Marjorie had to be cared for, as Father said in another letter, "I am always worried when I have to leave her with the hired girl.")

*　　*　　*

"Dear Sir: Your bill has been long overdue and I am desirous of getting a settlement. There are 15 visits charged to you amounting to $32.50. If you will pay me $15 any time during this month I will receipt your bill 'paid in full.'"

*　　*　　*

"Dear Maggie: Your letter came this morning. I am extremely sorry the doctor thinks there will be permanent injury to Dorothy's eyes. I will hasten down to you again as soon as Dr. Perkins comes to relieve me here and as soon as I can get my pass." (The Stickney family rated passes because my father had been designated a Northern Pacific Railroad physician.) "The snow is so dazzling that I have to wear smoked glasses. The pump has frozen up in the kitchen and I will have to thaw it out today for I used all the water there was pumped up taking a bath this morning. I am glad you are going to a private family to board. You will be able to get out more and to get a little enjoyment out of life. Yours, with my love."

* * *

"Dear Maggie: Dr. Perkins has not arrived and I have not received my pass yet. I just now got your letter telling me of your discovery of the ulcers. Where in her eyes are they located? What does Dr. McDevit say the trouble with the baby's eyes is? I feel so sorry she is not getting along better. I feel so sorry for you both. I hope the operation he contemplates will bring her complete relief. The storm continues here. The snow has banked so high around the house that I had to shovel my way out to get to the street. I have kept your two plants alive although they look pretty sickly. Yours, with my love."

* * *

"Dear Brother Will: . . . and for the support of our parents I can not send the whole amount at once. Thirty per cent of my stock died last winter and I am unable to command any cash except as I earn it. I have two beautiful children and my greatest pleasure is in the realization that they may not have the hardships I have encountered. This, of course, may make me over cautious."

* * *

(This next letter refers to a confinement case in the town of Taylor, which was a twenty-five-mile horseback ride from Dickinson.)

"Dear Madam: I am sorry your trouble is so prolonged, and I hope you will soon be entirely well again. Your bill is

$30—$20 for the confinement and $5 a visit for subsequent visits. I have cut the whole bill down $5, thus making it $30 in all. I am very much in need of money and if it is not inconvenient would like to have you send that amount. Hoping you and the baby are now in good health, I am, Sincerely yours."

* * *

"Dear Sir: Your bill has been a long time overdue and I am very desirous of having it settled. The balance due me amounts to $7.50."

* * *

"Dear Brother Will: Enclosed please find my check for $100. I had hoped to come East but it looks at present as though I would have to give up that pleasure."

* * *

"Dear Maggie: I have just returned from a call to Medora. Did not get much sleep and have just gotten up from a nap on the couch feeling quite refreshed. I have not received a bill from the hospital as yet. I do not like to take issue with authority, but I can not see for the life of me how that child can be in danger of blindness. I am worrying about what you are doing today and how you are getting along. Yours, with my love."

* * *

(He got to St. Paul and home again, for here is part of his next letter:)

"Dear Maggie: I got home this morning feeling well. The scarlet fever has a new hold here. Michael Lally's middle child and Guy de France's baby have died during my absence. I hope to get a letter from you today. I hated dreadfully to leave you there alone. Don't you think I had better ask Cousin May to come down and help you take care of the baby? The house is beginning to look like a stable since the muddy weather came on."

* * *

"Dear Sister Elizabeth: I am in hearty accord with our parents' golden wedding celebration. But it is doubtful if I will be able to participate. We have given up all other concerns to Dorothy's welfare. You see, the poor little thing has been in the hospital in St. Paul for the last seven months. She will not let anyone care for her but Maggie. Maggie left the hospital for a few hours one day while a nurse was in charge of Dorothy. The nurse had held the baby's nose to make her swallow medicine, with the result that her eyes were swollen shut for two days from crying. Maggie is so closely confined that I fear for her health as well. Everything is being done for the baby that skill and care can do, and we must hope for the best.

"Marjorie is just the sweetest child that ever lived. I will take her with me to visit her Mama and her little sister.

"It is possible I may take Dorothy on to New York to consult the best skill there. I have to work hard to keep ends meeting.

"No, I don't think either one of our children will be musical. Maggie and I are much disappointed as we both love music and used to dream of giving at least one of them a musical education, but they show no talent whatever. Nevertheless, we have two fine girls. Maggie will send photographs. Yours, with love."

* * *

"Dear Maggie: Marjorie has just brought in Dorothy's little rubber doll and insists on my sending it to her. She is delighted with the idea of Dorothy wearing black glasses and has never stopped talking about it to everyone she sees. I am glad you can now get out in the daytime with the baby. I hope her improvement will be rapid and permanent. You don't know how

I miss you and how your absence saddens me. My love for you grows stronger every day. How I wish I could see you and hold you in my arms today.

"I gave Marjorie a good scrubbing last night and put clean clothes on her this morning. She looks quite sweet in her little blue dress but I can not fix her hair so it will look pretty. The weather is beautiful today. If you were here we would hitch up the buckboard and take a drive to the pasture lot and have our luncheon on the grass. I dug up some woodbine from the banks of the Hart River to plant around the porch. The cottonwood saplings that I took from the Hart for you so long ago look sturdy, and have grown even since you were here. We will soon have a shady yard for the children to play in. Yours, with my love."

The childhood and growing-up years were a plaid pattern of bright and dark squares—literally as well as figuratively. The dark patches were, of course, when the old eye trouble recurred. The most bothersome part of that was my acute sensitivity to light. Outdoors I wore big round black glasses and deep sunbonnets that Mother had lined with something dark green. My very earliest memory is of playing on the floor of the parlor made really dark by blankets tacked over the windows. Even drawn shades could not sufficiently shut out the blazing prairie sunlight. Father's big medical books were fine for building houses, and Mother was always within reach, often sitting at her sewing machine just outside the parlor door.

Until I was sixteen the corneal ulcers plagued me intermittently, and at those times school, and life in general, was interrupted. Through the years there were trips to St. Paul or Boston for the necessary operations. There were seven in all. And Mother was always there to lead me or feed me or keep me company when the dark rooms got too boring. Perhaps one of the reasons I was so especially close to Mother was because she had done a most unusual thing for me. She had helped me to learn how not to cry. I learned it very early. Crying brought dire and immediate consequences. It aggravated the inflammation and made the pain worse, so it was terribly important to keep from crying about anything—not as a matter of bravery but of simple self-preservation. Mother helped me invent ways of quick diversion for emergencies. "Think hard about something nice. Think about Christmas. Think about your birthday. And keep busy doing, doing, doing things until the need to cry is over." And Mother had held me close day after day, night after night, and had invented splendid dreams for the future. Splendid things for me to think about, and I learned never to cry at all.

Even in dark rooms or with bandaged eyes the "Keep busy doing things" was possible—though limited. And I accomplished two things which turned out to be useful. I learned to typewrite by touch. Someone taught me the keyboard and I felt it out on Dad's big typewriter. For my twelfth birthday I was given a little portable Corona of my own, and from that day to this I have seldom written by hand, and my handwriting has remained that of a twelve-year-old. I learned to play the mandolin, and that also proved useful some years later when I went barnstorming through the small towns of North Dakota and Montana with a concert party of four girls called "The Southern Belles."

The "think about something nice" technique had no limits whatsoever. Besides the thinking about Christmas and birthdays, I could always transport myself to places where there were light and color and activity and music and a pink parasol to be carried in the sunshine—or to places where there were trees and brooks and lakes with water lilies such as I had seen on visits to Vermont, and where no wind ever whistled around the house or blew dust into one's eyes.

During the sojourns to St. Paul or Boston Dad would write me nonsense letters with jokes. And once he wrote a long Kiplingesque poem that began "Dear Long-Necked Dorothy" and ended "Destitute Dad." Here are the first and last verses:

> It's easy enough to be happy, my dear,
> When a girl is healthy and strong
> But the girl worthwhile
> Is the girl who can smile
> When her bally glims go wrong.

The test of a heart is its bruising
And it comes somehow with the years,
But the girl who can cause
Her Dad's applause
Is the girl who can smile through her tears.

The habit of not crying became so strong, so ingrained, that long after my eyes got well I was still not able to cry even when I most needed to. Mine was a childhood that lasted much longer than it should have. Lasted, in fact, until my mother's death. I couldn't cry even then.

I was fitted with thick-lensed glasses which were never taken off except for a bath or going to bed. I hated them passionately and longed to get rid of them.

But much of the time I was well and led the normal, happy life of any small-town child. My sister and I went to school, and in the afternoons when we rushed home and threw down our books, Mother was always there to answer to "Mother, I'm home!" We might find her at her sewing machine or in the kitchen fixing baked beans or frying doughnuts, with the little round part that came out of the center crisp and covered with sugar and waiting for us. She was pretty and merry and warm. The kind of mother who loved to create taffy pulls in the kitchen in winter or birthday parties on the lawn under the cottonwoods in summer. I loved her beyond anything or anyone in the world.

We were read to a lot. Dad read to please himself as well as us—Mark Twain, Stevenson, O. Henry, Dickens, while my sister and I lay on the floor listening and hoping no one would hear that loud-mouthed clock strike bedtime. I still have occasional *Oliver Twist* nightmares. Not because Bill Sykes murdered Nancy but because he kicked his faithful dog off the roof. That I have never forgiven. Mother read things like *The Five Little Peppers and How They Grew*. During the well times, when I could do my own reading, my tastes were varied. Flat on my stomach in the attic agonizing over Elsie Dinsmore, reading the *Oz* books, *The Little Colonel*, all the Frances Hodgson Burnett books, *St. Nicholas* magazine, and the books I filched from the red-leather set of Poe purposely put away on the top shelf behind the glass doors of Dad's bookcase.

But most exciting of all was my discovery of Victor Hugo when I was twelve or thirteen. Those were the nights when everyone else had gone to bed and I sat in the big leather chair in the bay window, with my feet on the radiator, and Buddy, the little fox terrier, asleep in my lap, and an enormous Victor Hugo book propped up against Buddy. It had dark woodcut-kind of illustrations that looked as though they might have been done by Doré; who knows, perhaps they were. Sometimes I would leave Jean Valjean or the Hunchback long enough to look out the window, and by the light of the corner street lamp watch the wind blow dust down the street and tear the circus posters off the building opposite. It was on these nights that I knew for certain, and perhaps for the first time with complete conviction, that I was going to get away from Dickinson as soon as I could.

And then there were the warm summer nights when the corner street lamp sifted light through our cottonwoods—now the biggest trees in town—and made dancing shadows as I sat on the top step of the porch on the big pillow that was stuffed with sweet-smelling straw and that rustled pleasantly when I moved. The cottonwoods had hard shiny leaves and they made a noise like rain. And there were the nights when I would slip out of the house and walk alone to the deserted depot just to smell the railroad tracks, with their lovely cindery, acrid smell and their hints of faraway places. And the many, many nights when from my bed I would hear the trains chug-chug into the station and chug-chug out again, leaving behind their long drawn-out wild whistles. Two short and one long repeated until the sound died away in the distance while I lay listening. "Who—who whooooooo!" they called, "Far—far awaaaaaay!" they promised. When Edna St. Vincent Millay wrote, "There isn't a train I wouldn't take no matter where it's going," she was speaking for hordes of small-town boys and girls who, like me, longed to find out what adventure was waiting at the end of the railroad tracks.

From the litter on the floor I rescued an album of childhood photographs, most of them taken by Mother: A picture of an early Christmas tree, with toys I still remember beneath it. A picture of Dorothy, naked except for a fold of cheesecloth draped around her protruding middle to match the cheese-cloth draped around the umbrella stand against which I was resting an elbow. With my fat stomach I look more like a kewpie than the Cupid which Mother had obviously intended. There was a picture of a birthday party of six-year-olds, little girls in white pinafores and with bows on their slippers, and little boys in Buster Brown collars. Oh, my midsummer birth-day was always lovely! There would be planks set up on sawhorses on the grass, in the shade of the cottonwoods, and little individual cupcakes that mother had frosted in different colors. And always there were the small yellow roses from the bush that grew beside the corral fence. Mother had brought it back from a Vermont visit, and it never failed to blossom for my birthday.

There is a picture of Marjorie and me on our Indian ponies which triggered a vivid memory of the first time I was ever on a horse. I must have been four or five years old. The horse was a big bay that Father rode—a very tall horse. I was lifted to the saddle and sat there miles above the ground, and pretty scared, while Dad walked ahead on the sidewalk leading us by the reins. After a block or so he gave the reins to me, and I rode proudly alone while way down on the ground Dad walked proudly beside us. When I was a few years older I had a little Indian pony of my own. Almost every child in town had one. Mine was a buckskin with black mane and tail, and his name, of course, was Buck. And when I pressed a certain spot on his spine just above the tail—he did. His heels would fly up like the donkey on those mechanical toy banks. The western saddle had a high horn and a high back, and since I was always prepared he never threw me. And how I loved to show off.

Once I rode my pony alone out on the prairie. It was a lovely day. I dropped the reins to the ground—no Indian pony ever needed to be hitched, just drop the reins over his head and he stayed put and cropped the grass. I lay down on my back in a little gully, or buffalo wallow, among some high prairie grass just because I felt like it—and looked at the sky. The sky was enormous—overpowering—and the earth was empty and the wind made a sound as it always did, and suddenly I was alone—the only person in the whole world, and I was frightened. I scrambled up, got on my pony, and galloped for dear life to home and safety.

We were a tough gang of outlaws then. My sister was "Rattlesnake Joe." I was "Panhandle Pete." Oh, and there was "Alkali Ike." I've forgotten which little girl he was. We used to race the cloud shadows across the prairie when the wind was blowing, and we tried to imitate the stunts we had seen at the circus. Picking up a handkerchief from the ground at a gallop, etc. We seldom used roads but cut across the plains to whatever destination we pleased, with nothing to stop us. Sometimes we had dawn picnics on the top of a butte, made coffee over a fire and watched the sun come up. In a certain place there were faint marks on the prairie grass that we had been told were Custer's Trail where the Seventh Cavalry had ridden on their way to the Battle of the Little Big Horn. Riding our ponies over that trail we must have felt a certain affinity for the Seventh Cavalry as we spent a lot of time trying to keep the trail open and visible. I have recently been reading about General Custer and have learned that when the massacre at Little Big Horn was over and the braves had left the field, the squaws went out and saw to it that every one of the dead men was mutilated beyond recognition, every one except Custer. His body was left untouched. A mark of respect to a white chief no doubt. Fort Lincoln, where the cavalry had been stationed, was only one hundred miles from Dickinson. It must have been a grand sight when the men rode out two abreast, in their blue uniforms, with yellow handkerchiefs tied around their necks and their hats turned up at the side—a line that could be seen for two miles across the prairie. The band always played when they went into battle, even on the plains with the Indians. "Gary Owen" was their official tune. And when they rode away from the fort the band always played "The Girl I Left Behind Me." And the girls they left behind often didn't know what had happened to their men until weeks later when a pony express would come their way.

Here I go again actually believing I was there. We rode over that trail and kept it visible for a few short years until the farmers came with their plows and their fences. After that, riding on roads between miles of barbed wires wasn't so much fun.

Dad's office had once been the back room of our house. It opened on a small porch with one door to his office and another door to the kitchen. The office was furnished with a rolltop desk, a lot of books, a glass case of instruments, an operating table covered with black leather, and a naked electric bulb that hung down from a cord in the middle of the ceiling. When the doctor needed more light for an operation, Mother supplemented the electric bulb by holding an oil lamp down close for him to see by. When it was over she would come out to the vine-covered porch and faint as quietly and unobtrusively as possible. I can see her clearly, leaning her back against the house wall and sliding down to the porch floor. I have been there when it has happened, but we never told Dad. I can also remember being startled awake by the telephone ringing at two or three in the morning and the sounds of Father going to the barn to saddle the horse or to hitch up the sleigh.

When my parents came to Dakota, Vermont came too. In the cellar there were always a barrel of apples, a large can of maple syrup, and a tin pail of maple sugar. They kept company with the shelves of homemade preserves and the huge bin of coal for the furnace. We had baked beans and brown bread every Saturday night, and codfish cakes on Sunday mornings, and sometimes wonderful buckwheat cakes dripping with maple syrup.

Sunday morning also meant going to mass. Father was not a Catholic so he didn't have to go. Confession and communion must have started when I was about eight. In my mind God and the Church were one and the same, with the priest running a close second. I had a blue prayer book with gold lettering on the cover, and I believed quite literally everything it said. In the "examination of conscience" part the prayer book told me: "I would rather DIE than ever again offend Thee." So I knelt in the dim, incense-smelling church for hours until I had flailed myself into believing I really would. I suffered quite a lot before daring to go into the confessional booth. It was never quite clear to me what was a mortal and what was a venial sin, so I took no chances and confessed everything I could think of. We had a nice priest who didn't scare me as much as God and the prayer book did. And in the confessional every time I paused in my recital of sins he would murmur, "Vaaaary good."

The whispered confession went something like this: "Bless me, Father, for I have sinned." "I was mean to my mother." "I didn't pay attention at mass." "I pinched my sister." "I had immodest thoughts." "I told a lie." At the end came the act of contrition which I knew by heart. "Oh, my God, I am heartily sorry for having offended Thee. And I detest my sins because I dread the loss of Heaven and the pains of Hell." And at the very end, "And I firmly resolve with the help of Thy Grace to confess my sins, do penance, and to amend my life." Then the priest would whisper back from his little slatted window, "Say five Our Fathers and five Hail Marys, like a good girl." After doing my penance I would skip out into the fresh air relieved and happy in the conviction that I would amend my life and that I would escaped hell one more time.

Mother, like many ladies of her period, painted china and did "studies" in oil. Everything in our house that could possibly be decorated was. We had "A Yard of Roses" over the dining-room door and "A Yard of Pansies" over the living-room door, and at the bottom of the pier glass in the parlor a water lily was painted. What has become of it all? Mother persistently planted her New England garden every spring— nasturtiums and sweet peas growing up the corral fence, and when the garden was destroyed by rust or hail or drought or grasshoppers, as it often was, she would stand behind her lace curtains looking out the bay window and cry, and vow she would never plant another garden, but she always did.

And then there was Christmas. Gay, glittery, shiny Christmas. The day the whole year led up to. For a week before the house was full of secrets and excitement and good smells, and on Christmas Eve the tree in all its glory. Colored wax candles lighted, and the tree festooned with the dear familiar ornaments and draped with the ropes of popcorn and cranberries we had strung by the kitchen stove the night before. And afterward, the walk to church for midnight mass with the air smelling of clean snow, and the stars popping out of the sky, and the snow squeaking under our overshoes, and the singing of "Holy Night," and "Oh, Come All Ye Faithful."

When all my silver was stolen there was only one thing that could never be replaced. It was the first non-homemade present that I had ever given my mother. A silver pie knife that I had admired in the window of Green's Jewelry Store on Front Street. That year, for the first time I had been given money to shop for presents. Five dollars. The pie knife cost four dollars and a half, and the rest of my list was taken care of with the remaining fifty cents. I had that pie knife until the burglars took it.

Dickinson, like most small towns, had an opera house. It had never housed an opera but the name sounded more respectable than "theatre." The *Uncle Tom's Cabin* shows came to town every summer as regularly as the circus and, like the circus, had street parades. It was deliciously exciting to hang over the fence and watch the glamorous company trail up the street past our house. Living on the corner of Sims and Main, we were in the thick of everything. Simon Legree would lead two very large dogs that were cast as bloodhounds, and Little Eva would ride by in her little painted chariot drawn by Shetland ponies. Her curls were always blond and her bonnet always plumed, and how I envied her. I also longed to be the lady in the pink tutu in the circus who rode bareback on a white horse.

Aside from the *Uncle Tom* shows my first two plays were *The Count of Monte Cristo* (who knows, Eugene O'Neill's father may have been played in it) and a musical called *The Mayor of Tokyo*. When they sang

"Tokyo, Tokyo beautiful at night
Like a brilliant firefly is every
tiny light"

and the stage was darkened and the chorus girls in Japanese kimonos swayed up and down with tiny lights on the spokes of their parasols it was pure magic. All I can remember of *The Count of Monte Cristo* was the terrifying lashing of canvas waves and a man behind prison bars calling, "Abbey Father! Father! Abbey!" Marjorie and I played it behind the bars of the dining-room chairs for weeks afterward.

We played show a lot in the attic or in the barn. It was usually something from a book of plays Louisa May Alcott had written for herself and her young sisters to act in. These plays all had a definite Shakespearean flavor, were pretty fancy tragedies, and were always in the doublet-and-hose period. We learned the dialogue by heart. The cast consisted of our playmate Marion, who was pretty and had glossy brown ringlets, Marjorie, who was snub-nosed and had a Dutch bob, and me, who was towheaded and wore glasses. In the attic there were always long dresses to trail around in and show clothes of various kinds, but our most prized piece of wardrobe was a pair of red silk stockings which Mother must once have used for some costume party. We took turns at them. On us they reached to the thigh, and with our black sateen bloomers pushed up as far as they would go, and our blue serge military capes with their red linings thrown dashingly over one shoulder, and our blue tam o' shanters trimmed with whatever plumes we could find in the millinery box, we could swashbuckle to our hearts' content. Marion refused to play anything but the heroine, and Marjorie insisted on being the villain, so that left me to be the hero, though I was a head shorter than either of them. Here is a sample of the dialogue that I remember without even trying:

VILLAIN (Marjorie) (*Entering on tiptoe*): Hist! All is still. They are not yet here. On this spot will the happy lovers meet, but I do vow vengeance on them for she did reject my suit for his. (*Hides behind tree.*)

Enter HEROINE *and* HERO (Marion and me)

HERO: Nay, dearest love, fear not. No mortal eye beholds us now and yon bright moon looks kindly down upon our love.

HEROINE: Ah, dearest Adelbert, with thee I feel no fear but thy fierce rival does vow vengeance on thee. Etc., etc., etc.

Anyway, we all died of poison in the last scene.

It became evident that I was not going to get much of an academic education as school was so often interrupted. But I wanted so much to keep up with the boys and girls my own age that I studied very hard and managed to skip the eighth grade of grammar school and enter high school when they did. This worked out badly because the old eye trouble returned. So it was decided that I was to go to a boarding school in St. Paul where I could take special courses that put no strain on my eyes, and where I would be near the eye specialist who had looked after me for so long. Special courses always turned out to be elocution, dancing, voice, physical culture—that sort of thing. But at least it made me feel that I was no different from the others because I was going to school too. While I was in this boarding school the ulcers started again and my eyes were swollen and red and must have looked pretty repulsive even behind my glasses. The girls started acting very strangely. They avoided me. Even my roommate, who had been my friend, threw open the window and kept to the far side of the room. I was hurt, but mostly bewildered. When I finally asked her why, she told me the horrid truth. I had some contagious disease and they were all afraid of catching it. As far as I knew it might have really been true, so I ran to the doctor and asked him. He assured me that what I had I couldn't possibly give away. I think he may also have phoned the school authorities, for things got better after that. By this time it was midwinter. We all went home for the holidays, and I was not able to go back to school.

Mother as a bride

My father

Dickinson, N. Dak. in 1882.

Dickinson, North Dakota, as my father first saw it (LAWTON OSBORN)

My father making his calls (LAWTON OSBORN)

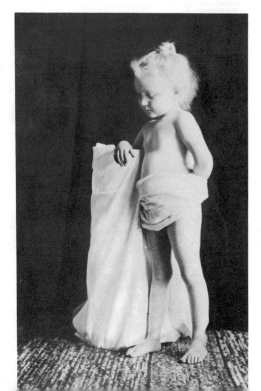

My mother took this
photograph of me

Howard selling his uncle's
papers on the Boardwalk

With my cousin and sister in
Vermont (MRS. VICTOR STICKNEY)

In my party clothes (OSBORN STUDIOS)

My sister, Marjorie, and me (OSBORN STUDIOS)

The family on holiday

"The Southern Belles"

Taken shortly after my arrival in New York (LEWIS SMITH)

That was my last bout with the old eye trouble. From then on my eyes started to get well. The curious thing is that to this day no one seems to know what caused it in the first place or why it ended. If there was a name for it I was never told. I still wore the hated glasses, but no more corneal ulcers ever.

Two years later I went to another school to take more "special courses." It was a Catholic college and stands out in my memory for three special reasons. The most important reason was Sister Charitas who taught dramatic art and whom I loved very dearly. She had reddish eyebrows, so we assumed there must be red hair under her wimple, and we called her Sister Carrots behind her back. Lovely Sister Carrots and I corresponded regularly until she died, a very old lady in retirement.

The second important thing was "the retreat." As a child I had not been sent to a parochial school, nor had I any intimate acquaintance with priests or nuns, so I was not really prepared for some of the customs of a Catholic school, certainly not for a retreat. A retreat meant getting up at six in the morning for the earliest mass, attending several sessions through the day, keeping absolute silence—one must not even whisper—and in silence and devotion we were to purify our souls. The only one who should have kept silent and didn't was the priest who conducted the affair. He happened to be the revivalist type. At the earliest mass he dangled us over hell's fire until we could positively feel the heat. He drew vivid pictures of our mothers lying dead in their coffins before us, and weren't we sorry and ashamed that we had ever been unkind or selfish or cross with her. I left the chapel shaken. I went back to my room in silence, found that last week's allowance had not been spent, put on my brand-new suit and hat, walked out the gate, and took the first streetcar to St. Paul. I lunched at the tearoom that one's parents took one to on visits, saw a vaudeville show in the afternoon, had dinner at night in solitary elegance at a restaurant where they played music, went to another vaudeville show that evening, came back to school about eleven, and found the poor nuns wringing their hands. I kept silent during the next two days, but I didn't go back to church until retreat was over and I could start being a good Catholic again.

The third important thing happened one day after I had broken both my pairs of glasses and had gone to the doctor for another prescription. When I was quite young I had started asking how long must I wear them, the answer had always been: "A few more years, a few more years." This time I begged the doctor to tell me truly how long it would be. His answer was, "Don't be silly, child, you will have to wear them all your life." That did it. On my way back to school I tore up the prescription and threw it out the streetcar window. For the first couple of weeks without glasses I stumbled dizzily around, holding on to furniture, but my eyes gradually came into focus again, and I saw at least as well as I had ever seen from behind those thick lenses. And my eyes continued to get well. The fact that my vision has been impaired is something that I made an adjustment to so long ago that I can't even remember. I have felt no deprivation whatever, and no one but an eye specialist can see the scars.

Sister Charitas must somehow have pointed me in the right direction because the next year I went to a small drama school in Minneapolis. She must also have given me a head start because they let me finish in one year instead of the prescribed two. I had never graduated from anything before. Now I was going to graduate in June. Life was beautiful. I was radiantly happy. I knew what I wanted. I wanted to learn to act. I wanted to be in the theatre. How to go about it was a mystery, but I knew where I was going. This was the adventure at the end of the railroad tracks.

In my memory of that June it is always nighttime—warm, soft, fragrant nighttime—that festive week when I graduated from school in Minneapolis. I am wearing a pink organdy dress and a leghorn hat with a pink rose and blue streamers. I am being courted by a young officer just back from the war. He wears a Sam Browne belt and medals and shiny boots and a jaunty overseas cap. We go dancing in hotel dining rooms to the music of "Dardanella" and "Just a Love Nest." He sends me roses and takes me driving around the lakes in a rented car, and there is always a full moon. When we have finished saying good night I go up to my bedroom and undress without turning on the lamp. There is an oblong of blue moonlight on the floor, and the world smells of lilacs and tastes of happiness.

I took the midnight train for Dickinson. All trains were adventures, but a midnight train was best of all. The lovely acrid, cindery smell, the long wail of the whistle, the clicketty-clack-clack of the ties underneath as you went to sleep in your berth, and the promise of something unknown and wonderful at the end of any journey, even though the journey was toward rather than away from home. The young officer came to see me off, bringing a box of candy and a leather-bound, gold-lettered book of *The Rubaiyat* with colored illustrations by Dulac. He boarded the train just so we could ride together to the next station because everything was joyous and beautiful and we didn't want it to end. But the berths were made up and the car was dark, and there was no place to sit, so we stood in the swaying, clattering vestibule between the cars and held hands while the warm June night flew past the open window. Finally we said a reluctant good-bye. He got off at some town, the train pulled out, with two long and two short whistles, and I waved to him standing under a light on a deserted station platform. Then I climbed into my berth and opened the box of candy and *The Rubaiyat*.

My parents couldn't come East for graduation because Mother was not well. Dad had written me that she would have to stay in bed for a while. But I was surprised on getting home to find that we had a nurse staying in the house. She was a nice girl, whose family we knew and whom my father had helped through training school. On the whole, I was glad she was there to do extra things for Mother until she was up and around again.

That last week had had the quality of a romantic dream, and I loved thinking about it, but still, it was good to be home. Home was dear dependable reality. Home was most specifically Mother. Dad too, of course, but that was a shade different. Dad was a kind and scholarly man who could be taciturn in the reserve that was natural to his New England background. That, and the fact that a hardworking country doctor must be away from home much of the time, had made him seem a little remote. Mother was not scholarly and never remote. She was the confidant and the adored best friend. During the frequent periods of sitting in dark rooms or with bandaged eyes, when I couldn't go to school or skate or play basketball or go to parties like my older sister, Mother had always been there. We would find things to giggle about, and she would read me books, or make a new dress for my doll or for me, and, in general, cushion the bad things and make the good ones better. She was pretty and gay and warmly loving, and just now, she was quite unreasonably proud of her homecoming child.

Of course there was much to be talked over—graduation, my new beau, oh, lots of things. But most exciting was the surprise Mother had been saving up for me. We were going to remodel the old house! She and Dad had even thought of building a new one, but that would have meant leaving our yard with the big cottonwood trees, the ones they had dug up as saplings from the river bank and had planted around the house the first year they were married. Now our cottonwoods were the biggest trees in town.

On that first night at home my sister and her new husband had supper with us. He was the young doctor from Wisconsin who had come to take over the medical practice when Father retired. He stayed in the kitchen with my sister and me while we did the dishes. I said, "Tell me honestly, Bob, how long do you think it will be before Mother is well again?" He said, "She isn't going to get well." I said, "What do you mean?" He repeated, "She isn't going to get well." I stared stupidly and asked again, "What do you mean?" And then he said, "Your mother isn't going to get well. She is going to die."

I put down the dish towel on the zinc-topped table and walked out the kitchen door into the back yard. Father passed me, coming in from the garage. I didn't really see him but I heard him say, "Oh!" And then, "I didn't want them to tell you." I sat down on the grass, back of the old windmill. It was covered with woodbine and hid me from the house and from the street. I was numb and frozen. Perhaps it was minutes or perhaps it was hours later when Father put his hand on my shoulder. "You'd better come in, dear, and say good night to Mother. She mustn't know." I got up and went to her bedroom. I said, as always, "Good night, Mother. I love you."

Upstairs I shut my bedroom door and sat in the little rocking chair facing the window. I couldn't cry. My middle felt hard and petrified. There was only an enormous, enveloping ache and the numbness. People passed by on the sidewalk below, laughing and talking, on their way to the movies or the ice-cream parlor. It seemed very strange when the world had just ended. The door must have been opened and closed at intervals through the night, but I didn't hear. Toward morning I was dimly aware that someone got me into bed.

Mother looked particularly pretty the next day—her hair so black, her eyes such bright, bright blue, and her teeth so very white when she laughed. We started at once to plan the house. We would have a modern kitchen like the ones pictured in our magazines, and our extra bathroom would have colored fittings, and we would add a whole room on the side of the house where there were no trees. Dad came in and sat on the edge of the bed. He had brought a bunch of the little lemon-scented yellow roses from the bush in our garden. He suggested that we might even put in a fireplace too. We agreed that it was a fine idea, and Mother, propped up on her pillows, looked young and happy.

After a while she no longer used her upstairs room. The parlor was turned into a bedroom for her. We had brought down the big brass bed and the bird's-eye maple dresser, with her silver brush and comb set, and the photographs and snapshots stuck in the mirror frame, and the little bird's-eye maple rocking chair. The parlor was nearer the bathroom and the kitchen, and on the rare days when she was well enough to sit up she loved sitting among her pillows in the big chair in the living room.

She grew steadily worse. I wonder if she knew or guessed

the seriousness of her illness. She had clipped a little verse from a magazine and had attached it to the head of her bed. It said—

> This little strip of light twixt night and night,
> Let me keep bright today,
> And let no shadow of tomorrow or sorrow of dead yesterday
> Gainsay my happiness today;
> And if tomorrow should be sad, or never come at all,
> I've had at least today.

These were the words she lived by until the stroke came and delirium took over.

My sister was living in her own home and looking after her husband. Father and the nurse and I cared for Mother. She was delirious for four weeks before she died, and talked continually night and day—just words, no meaning. Often she would repeat the name of someone from her childhood. And sometimes—oh, this was the most terrible of all—she would call for me to come to her when I would be right there all the time, holding her tight in my arms, and saying close in her ear, "Mother darling, I am right here. I am right here with you. Please—please—PLEASE know that I am here." I would often even turn on the bright ceiling light in the frantic hope that she would see me and know me—trying desperately to reach her mind and never getting beyond that awful wall of delirium.

Scott Fitzgerald once said, "In the night of the soul it is always three o'clock in the morning." It is also four o'clock. Five is not quite so black and hopeless because you know that in one more hour it will be six and the world will start coming alive again. Mother died on Christmas Eve. I knew it would happen on that particular night. I don't know how I knew, but I did. The priest and the altar boys arrived to perform the last rites, what is known in the Church as "extreme unction." They lighted candles by her bed and chanted in Latin. I sat on the top step of the stairway just outside my bedroom and listened. I remember very little else.

There are blank spaces in the following days. I succeeded in blotting out the funeral service and the trip to the cemetery so completely that I cannot bring it back to mind even now. I remember the sound of the church bells tolling and I remember Father saying, "Please come in and look at her, Dorothy. You will be glad you did. She looks so peaceful and pretty."

The bedroom had been turned back into the parlor and her casket was there. I went in with Dad and looked down at her face. She did look beautiful and peaceful as if she was about to smile. People kept saying, "Why don't you cry, dear. You will feel better if you cry." I couldn't. My body felt like a block of cement. I was encased in a hard shell of desolation. Nothing moved.

After that, and after I had gone through the clothes in her closet, and ached over the little kid gloves that still smelled of her, and bore the imprint of her hands, I wanted to run. I ran and ran and never stopped running. I dared not stop. The only place I could think of to run to was back to school in Minneapolis. In the selfishness of my grief I never gave a thought to my father in his grief and loneliness. He was understanding, as always. He paid my way back to school where I would take a postgraduate course in something or other—in anything, it didn't matter.

I spent the mornings in school and in the afternoons I ran to a vaudeville show—there was always vaudeville playing somewhere. Then I ran back to my boardinghouse for something to eat and then ran to another theatre in the evening, always alone. I must not feel, I must not think, I must block out everything or it would be true, and I couldn't let it be true.

One night while I was watching a performance at the Orpheum Theatre I must have fainted. I woke up in a hospital, not having the slightest idea how I got there. Someone must have called an ambulance. I was in an operating room—and something was being done to my ears. Just before the anesthetic reached me I heard a voice say, "My God, it's a double abscess!" I had been having the flu and didn't know it. Both my ears were badly abscessed as a result. For the next four weeks I was deaf—totally, stone deaf. I can tell you from experience that being deaf is much worse than being blind. It is a feeling of complete and utter isolation, much more lonely than being without sight. My sister came to the hospital to visit me. I could see her but couldn't hear her. We had no way of reaching each other. It really didn't matter much that she was there. When I got better I went back to my boardinghouse because I didn't want to go home again—ever. I was still deaf, and I had been forced to stop running. In a matter of time my hearing returned, and I got well and went back to school. I was young and resilient, and most of the time I kept the door tight shut on the past months.

Occasionally I thought of the young officer who had been my beau that magical June when I had graduated a year before. But he was a civilian now and working in South America. (Civilians were not as romantic as soldiers just back from war.) I treasured the *Rubaiyat* he had given me and knew it all by heart, but our letters grew fewer and farther between, and my memory of him grew dimmer and dimmer. It was spring. I loved my work in school and happiness often overtook me.

When school closed a piece of good luck came my way, which solved the problem of my facing summer in a house without Mother. I was invited to join "The Southern Belles" to go on tour. This was a company of four girls who had graduated from school the year before, had given themselves a name, and had spent the previous summer playing the boondocks of the Middle West. One of the girls had dropped out and they wanted me for a replacement. I jumped at the chance. An advance man, whom we never saw, booked us into small towns, towns with such names as Cutbank, Whitefish, Lemon, and Rosebud.

The company consisted of Lee, who was the manager and who played violin, and who was surely the most talented among us, Laura, who played piano and was the prettiest—she had very white skin and black hair in a curly bob and was rather vain of her looks, and there was Helen who was also pretty but didn't know it. She was entirely disinterested in her appearance, and if her slip showed or if she had a run in her stocking, she couldn't have cared less. Helen played the drums. I played the mandolin. Helen and I sang, danced, and recited, always in costume. Among other things, we did child impersonations with songs shamelessly borrowed from Irene Franklin's vaudeville act.

We started in May in the town of Minot in northernmost North Dakota. Our boardinghouse had no indoor plumbing, and we were provided with basin, water pitcher, and a "convenience." The first morning we woke to find the water had frozen in the pitcher and we had to break a film of ice before we could wash our faces. I share memories of Minot with a man who many years later became my close friend. Boris Karloff had also played Minot in his early days in the theatre when his name was William Pratt, and long before the movies had discovered him. He had been a member of a stock company which played there for two whole seasons because they never had money enough to get out. We were luckier than Boris. Thanks to help from home we were able to move on the following day.

We were "The Southern Belles," though I doubt that any of us had been farther south than South Dakota, but when we were costumed in hoop skirts, ruffles, and fans, we must have thought we justified our name. We played for dances after the show if anyone wanted us to. It was a glorious lark and we reveled in it.

There was only one time when we got really terrified. Cutbank, Montana, was a railroad division point where the trains changed crews. The town actually had a hotel and we were terribly pleased when we got two adjoining rooms on the first floor. We arrived there a day before the performance. It was mid-July and boiling hot. What we didn't notice until night was that our windows opened on an alley, and men kept walking by and looking in. Men also knocked on our doors all night long, inviting us to come out and have a drink or to let them come in and have a good time with us. We were scared. So scared that we locked the windows, pulled down the shades, bolted our doors, and shoved chests of drawers against them. We huddled together all night—four of us in one bed, in the stifling heat, not daring even to take our clothes off or to turn out the lights. The next day we gave our performance, got out of town, and told each other that we were professionals, and that this was all part of being actresses on a road tour.

Another place we played—I have happily forgotten its name—was a mining town which also had a hotel, of sorts. The miners slept there in day-and-night shifts. One man got out of a bed and another man got into it. The hotel spared us two rooms that smelled as though they had been unremittingly occupied for years. There were bedbugs. That was the time Laura decided to sit up in the railroad station all night rather than sleep there. Lee and Helen and I sprayed the beds with perfume, making them much worse, of course, and slept among the bugs. We must have been awfully tired.

Our young self-confidence was enormous and only once was it badly shaken. When we got to Whitefish we had competition. There was a band concert in town that night and nobody came to see us. Not a single solitary soul. Even the janitor disappeared as soon as he had let us into the concert hall. We got made up and dressed, and peeked hopefully through the curtain for an hour before we finally gave up. Then we cleaned our faces, took off our hoop skirts, and trailed back to our boardinghouse, telling ourselves that "in the profession one must expect some setbacks."

We finished the tour at the end of summer, said our sad good-byes, and returned to our various homes.

———

When Father suggested that we take a trip East to visit our relatives my first thought was that Tyson, Vermont, couldn't possibly be too far from New York City, and New York City was where one had to go to be an actress.

Tyson is a village of white clapboard houses clustered at the edge of Echo Lake, a jewel of clear water dropped down in the middle of the Green Mountains. Uncle Will, who was then governor of Vermont, still owned the farm where the Stickney children grew up. He had remodeled and improved the house and barns until they were now the governor's summer home and the pride of the community. We spent two lovely, lazy weeks there visiting with aunts, uncles, and cousins, swimming, walking in the pine woods, or rowing on the still lake and picking water lilies.

Dad was willing for me to try New York. He would give me some money for expenses and my fare there and back to Dickinson. Did he perhaps think that the best way to get me home was to let me find out firsthand how lonely a big city could be? I was to go to the Woodstock Hotel because it was run by a man from Vermont and would therefore be a safe place for his daughter.

I arrived by train on an evening in early autumn, just at dusk when the sky was purple and all the city lights were beginning to blossom. At the Woodstock Hotel I leaned out my high window and watched with wonder as the huge Wrigley Gum sign flashed on and off. Across the street was Henry Miller's Theatre with a lighted sign on the marquee proclaiming "BLANCHE BATES IN THE FAMOUS MRS. FAIR." That night I saw my first New York play from the last row in the second balcony. I was less impressed with Blanche Bates, the star, than I was with the ingenue, beautiful, blond Margalo Gillmore. She was what I wanted to be. To this day I can remember clearly a little red feather hat she wore and how she ran across stage. I promised myself I would be exactly like that someday.

The next day I explored Broadway. It was best of all when evening came. The Broadway I saw on that early autumn evening was very unlike the tawdry street it is today. It was as gaudy and incandescent as it is now, but in those days it had its own special kind of elegance. I walked past fine restaurants and handsome theatres, and I saw beautiful ladies and top-hatted gentlemen on their way to dine or to see a play. I walked up and down Broadway, solitary but feeling important and exhilarated, and very much a part of the scene. I explored side streets where grimy shop windows displayed such treasures as wigs and makeup, toe slippers and ballet costumes, and yards of spangled cloth of every color to be used for Lord knew what glamorous purpose. All of it was perfect! The trolley cars rattled and banged, and the elevated roared, and I adopted New York for my very own. It didn't adopt me but I adopted it. And I knew without the slightest doubt that for better or for worse, sink or swim, succeed or fail, I was in New York for keeps.

Living in a hotel was far too expensive. Dad thought I should rent a room in some nice boardinghouse, but I didn't know how to go about finding one. I had never heard there were such places as endowed clubs—the Rehearsal Club, the Three Arts Club—where girls on their own could live inexpensively. I didn't even know about YWCAs. So, after four days at the Woodstock, I answered a newspaper advertisement: "Apt.—Will share . . ."

I told my prospective landlady a great big lie. I told her I was an actress—and she let me move in. It was a one-room and kitchenette apartment, with an alcove large enough to hold a cot, a chest of drawers, and my small trunk. The lady slept on a pull-out sofa bed in the living-room part. She was pretty, though terribly old, probably all of thirty or thirty-five. Her hair was bobbed, curly, and bright red. Her clothes weren't anything special, but she had beautiful filmy nightgowns and beautiful negligees trimmed with marabou, and beautiful underthings—black lace ones, even. Occasionally she packed a bag and went away for a night or two. She was amiable enough, but somehow we could never seem to get really well acquainted.

After having invented for myself an impressive background as to my theatre experience, I started looking for work. The classified phone directory made it easy to find addresses of producers and agents, and every day I made the rounds. The outer offices were crowded with actors and actresses of every shape and size. They waited and smiled and chattered together exchanging gossip—who was casting what play—and waited and smiled some more. How I longed for the day when I might join in.

Then, one afternoon two men came through the inner door of an agent's office and scanned the hopeful group. One pointed in my direction and said, "You." I looked around to see who he meant.

"You," he said, "the blond one." He consulted the other man. "She's the type all right." And there I was, after only two weeks in New York, engaged to play the ingenue in a dramatic act for vaudeville. The sketch had three characters. The other two would be played by the men. Later, I learned that they were a juggling and dance team who, having gotten tired of opening the show, had decided to move into a higher echelon with a twenty-minute drama which they themselves had written. I thought it superb; though it has since occurred to me that their juggling and dancing may have been better.

I wired Dad the glorious news. I was an actress and my salary was thirty-five dollars a week, or anyway it would be as soon as the act started playing. The men didn't know exactly when that would be, but, taking no chances, I bought my costume right away, a dress I had admired in a window on my evening walk down Broadway. It was white lace, with a red velvet ribbon around the waist and a big pink rose, and it cost twenty-five dollars. As things turned out, there was no great hurry after all because we rehearsed intermittently for nine weeks. During that time I didn't have much luck getting acquainted with the men either, but I was an eager rehearser and nine weeks didn't seem a bit too long.

This was a new world, a stimulating anything-can-happen sort of place, entirely unrelated to any world I had known before. It made Dickinson, North Dakota, seem so remote that at times it hardly existed. I was beginning to learn the technique of shutting out the things it was better not to remember. It worked quite well except for those moments that caught me unguarded, like seeing something in a shop and thinking, "That would look lovely on Mother." But now it was nearly Christmas and the technique didn't work so well. Holiday sights and sounds were everywhere, dazzling displays in windows, Salvation Army Santas on corners, familiar hymns and carols accompanied by wheezy organs, and being wakened in the morning by a German band on the street below thumping out "Tannenbaum" or "Stille Nacht." I tried to close eyes and ears, but Christmas had begun to creep in around the edges.

Then—the act was booked for a tryout, the last half of a split week at the Myrtle Avenue Theatre in Brooklyn. Four performances a day, and the dates would be December 23, 24, and 25. Four lovely performances a day and the long subway ride to Brooklyn and back. I could slip through Christmas and come out on the other side as if it hadn't happened.

I packed the white lace dress and the new makeup in its new metal makeup box, boarded the subway and arrived at the Myrtle Avenue station two hours before the front of the house opened. At the end of a dirty alley was a door marked "Stage Entrance." Back of it was a pitch-black passageway with a horrible smell. Lugging my suitcase I groped forward and collided with something that made a terrifying noise. It was a cage of seals.

The audience was sparse that afternoon, but in the evening there was a much larger and rowdier crowd. They began applauding, surprisingly, right in the middle of our act. At least I took it for applause. It was a rhythmic clapping—clap, pause, clap, pause, clap, pause, and the audience was doing it in unison. I wasn't aware that this was a form of criticism. After the last performance one of the men came to my dressing room with the bad news. The manager had canceled our act. He wouldn't even let us finish out the week.

The day of Christmas Eve it snowed. The men phoned in the morning to tell me that they were abandoning the act and I needn't come to rehearsals any more. About noon my landlady put on her hat and coat and said casually, "Well, goodbye, kid, I am going to get drunk over Christmas. See you in a few days." I was too scared even to be shocked. I didn't know the lady very well, but I didn't know anyone else at all, and Christmas Eve had to be gotten through. That would be the worst because up until last year it had always been the best—the lovely, luminous, best, most important day of the whole year.

I waited in the hall downstairs for the last mail delivery of the day—the one that would surely bring word from home—Christmas cards, a letter, and of course the box from Dad and my sister with presents and homemade candy and cookies. But the postman came and went and there was nothing. He explained about the blizzard in the West that had delayed all the mails.

Now it was dark and still snowing great, dry, fluffy flakes. The city was white and sparkling like a mica-covered greeting card. I could no longer keep Christmas at bay. The aloneness engulfed me. I couldn't cry because the ache in my throat was too hard and the knot in my middle too tight. Panic set in. I was going down for the third time. I yanked on overshoes, lunged into coat and hood, ran down the block, streaked up the stairs to the elevated, and headed for Broadway where there were people.

At Times Square the lights glittered on sifting snow in the air and powdery snow underfoot. There were gay people everywhere—people in couples, people in parties, people with other people. I felt shamefully conspicuous. I joined a laughing group, walking as close as I dared, trying to look as though I belonged to them. I followed them to a theatre entrance where a big sign blazed out "MITZI HAJOS—IN LADY BILLY." I bought a single seat. The orchestra was tuning up as I walked in elaborately consulting my watch, looking about and shaking my head in annoyance, as if the friend I expected was late in arriving. It was warm inside and the air was pervaded with that unique theatre smell and sound of an audience looking forward to a performance. The overture played, the lights dimmed, the house quieted and the curtain rose, and then—the magic gradually happened. Mitzi Hajos, Lady Billy, of course, disguised as a boy, sang and danced and made jokes that surprised me into laughing. The knot in my stomach began to loosen. I was not, after all, going down for the third time. I was safe and sheltered on a little island of light and music and color. And I was not alone. The actors, the audience, and I were somehow companions sharing the particular experience that is theatre. At intermission most of the people walked to the lobby and I sat still, but my throat didn't ache any more and I waited, comforted, for the next act to begin.

When the final curtain had shut me out, once again I edged close to a group and scuffed my way through the soft snow to the elevated. There were few passengers that night. The right-angled seats in the center of the car were empty. I sat close in the corner of one and turned my face to the snowy window, and then I cried. I cried my way back to the 86th Street Station, to the empty apartment and to sleep. The lump inside me had dissolved and Christmas Eve was over.

Fifteen years later I was again in a theatre on Christmas Eve, but this time I was on the other side of the footlights. The year was 1939. The play was the now legendary *Life With Father*. The theatre was the Empire, rich in tradition, and elegant in crimson and gold and crystal. Mine was one of the two names in lights over the marquee. The other was that of my husband, Howard Lindsay. He had written the play in collaboration with our dear friend, Russel Crouse. Now, Howard and I were acting in it together—joyously being husband and wife onstage as well as off. We had been married for twelve years.

On the morning of December 24 I woke up with a nasty case of the flu. The doctor said, "Phone her understudy. Of course she can't go on tonight." I knew better. There had been a few occasions when I had missed a performance because of illness, and the play had gone on unflatteringly well without me. But this was different. Howard was baffled at my stubborn insistence on getting up. He protested vehemently. It did no good. I couldn't explain even to myself just why it was so important to me to be there on this particular night, but it was.

Backstage was gay with tinsel balls and wreaths on doors, and bright packages piled up in dressing rooms. And I was there in the lovely white lace costume with its bustle and train, shaky in the knees but radiantly happy in the heart.

"Endearing" is a good word to describe *Life With Father*. It was an endearing play about a home and a family. It was believable and tender and gloriously funny, and a delight to look at with its sumptuous Victorian set and beautiful costumes. That night there seemed to be a special shine about the place, a special warmth in the audience, a special quality in their laughter and in their silences.

At intermission the company manager, who knew about my flu, came backstage to see how things were going. We chatted a few minutes. I asked the usual "How's the house?" and got the hoped-for reply, "Great! Sold out! Standees!" He turned to leave, then stopped in the dressing-room doorway and said, "Funny thing, we sold a lot of single seats tonight."

The final curtain fell and rose. The last bows were taken. I stepped to the footlights and said, "With all my heart I wish a Happy Christmas to every single person here!"

———

Only a few weeks ago I was being interviewed for a newspaper piece about *Pippin*, the very "mod" musical I was currently playing in. The first question was "How do you feel about nudity in the theatre?" And before I could think of an answer, "When you first started, when you were very, very young and desperately needed a job, and the job depended on your taking off your clothes, would you have done it?"

Well, in those far-off days I was so eager to get a toehold in the theatre that I might have done anything. However, with my first job it was not so much a matter of what I could take off as of what I could put on. That was what the job depended on and I knew it.

My first summer in New York I was, as usual, haunting all the theatrical offices looking for work. On this particular hot and humid day I was standing in the outer office of the Wales Winter Casting Agency among a lot of other perspiring hopefuls, wishing I knew any of them well enough to speak to. I was skinny—somewhere around ninety pounds, and built along the lines of Twiggy. But dresses were nearer the ankle than the knee in those days, and I was wearing a pretty new one of pale green organdy that looked cool and covered quite a lot of me.

A man came through the door of the inner sanctum, looked us all over, walked across to me, and said, "Can you wear tights?" I gasped, "Oh yes! I never have but I will! I'd like to!" He told me to go to a certain theatre where Leo Ditrichstein, the great European star, was casting the Chicago company for his starring vehicle called *Toto*. He needed two young Folies Bergère girls for the party scene in his gay and glamorous Paris apartment. He gave me a casual glance and the job.

Although my part consisted of only one line, it could truthfully be called the title role because my line was "Oh, Toto." I was to come dancing on in my flesh-colored tights, throw my arms around the star, cry joyously, "Oh, Toto," and dance off.

We were told to come back in September when the company would be taken to Chicago, would rehearse two weeks, and would have one dress rehearsal the night before the opening. I was in heaven! A part in a real play with a famous star! I was an actress at last!

In the meantime, we were sent to a costumer to be fitted out as Folies Bergère girls. My costume was adorable; a gold bodice and little red chiffon pants made like a basket, with flowers spilling out on each hip. The fittings were supervised by an assistant stage manager who didn't pay much attention. I was all right on top, but below I was not. My legs were terribly, terribly thin and the tights wrinkled. If anyone noticed I would lose the job, but no one did except the other girl. She said, "Those tights look wrinkly on you. Why don't you get some symmetricals?"

Symmetricals, I learned, were what Shakespearean actors wore when their legs were less than perfect. They were rather like long underwear, including feet, and they were padded in the right places to make up for what the legs lacked. Tights were pulled on over them and, behold, fine legs.

Symmetricals were made at a place in Brooklyn and could be ordered by sending one's measurements and twenty-five dollars. I was assured that the package would be mailed to me and would be there well before the dress rehearsal date. In Chicago I waited anxiously and checked every mail delivery at my boardinghouse.

The day of the dress rehearsal came and the symmetricals did not. I frantically phoned the Brooklyn firm and was told that they had been sent, must already be in Chicago, and would surely be in the next delivery. Too late!

I flew to a taxi and told the driver this was an emergency and he must take me to the main post office, fast. Fortunately he knew where it was. I demanded to see the head postmaster. A kind-faced man appeared and I told him, through a Niagara of tears, that I was an actress and that *my* play was to open *that night,* and that there was a very important package in *his* post office, and that the play could not possibly open without it, and would he please look through all the packages and find it—*please.* Whatever else he thought, he recognized tragedy when he saw it. He gave an order and about half an hour later the package was found.

I raced back to the theatre. The symmetricals fitted perfectly and my legs looked lovely in tights, dimpled knees and all. And Mr. Ditrichstein never knew they were not my own when I tripped on to the stage and said, "Oh, Toto."

Yesterday I came across a photograph from that play. My legs really did look grand, but I have just noticed they did not quite match my arms.

Getting back to the interview. If my job had depended on nudity what would I have done? I really don't know. The question just never came up.

———

After the *Toto* company closed I came back to New York and shared a rickety bedroom in a rickety West Side rooming house with another aspiring actress named Millie Beland. She was tiny and played child parts when she could get them. We wore out our shoes making the rounds of the offices every day. On summer nights when our bedroom was too stiflingly hot for sleeping, we would get seats in the open air on the top of a beautiful double-decker Fifth Avenue bus, and for ten cents each, we would ride all night and get a small breeze.

About three in the morning, when it got a little cooler, we would go back to our room and stretch out on the lumpy bed until it was time to get up and start looking for jobs again. We were hopelessly stagestruck. We pounded the pavements, and haunted managers' and agents' offices only to be turned away with a shake of the head, when we had barely gotten inside the door, or with "Nothing today," or, worst of all, with a "You're not the type." Life was a combination of hope and despair.

For three years I tried to see the producer Edgar Selwyn and never got further than his office boy. One day while waiting endlessly, hoping for a few words with the great man, I whiled away the time and vented my anger by writing some verses.

YOU'RE NOT THE TYPE

I looked for work in early fall
And could not find a part at all.
I looked and looked and looked and then
I looked and looked and looked again,
And looked and looked and now it's spring,
And still I haven't anything.
Too fat, too thin, too short, too tall,
Too blond, too dark, too large, too small.

An office boy my dream would thwart,
"You're not the type," I'd hear him snort,
So then I asked a big producer,
"Oh, let me play a part for you, sir!"
And as my eye he saw me wipe,
He yawned and said, "You're not the type."
A playwright next I interviewed,
My heart with brightest hopes imbued.

He turned away and lit his pipe,
And shortly said, "You're not the type."
To see an agent then I went,
My shoes worn out, my money spent.
The agent smiled and said, "My dear,
You're not the type. Come in next year,
For doubtless then we'll be engaging."
And I departed madly raging.

So here within my furnished room,
At least I face my awful doom.
I'll starve and go (I hope) above,
And this is what I'm thinking of—
Perhaps if I am very good
And play my harp as angels should,
Saint Peter will be kind to me
And lend me once his Golden Key.

I hope to see upon the stair
Imploring for admittance there,
Producers, playwrights, agents, too,
And all the deadly office crew.
When my familiar face they see
They'll say, "Don't you remember me?"
Then from the Pearly Gates I'll pipe,
"Oh, go to Hell! You're not the type!"

Toward the end of summer Millie got work playing a child
in a vaudeville act, and I got a job as ingenue in a stock company in New Bedford, Massachusetts. The New Bedford
Players had nothing at all in common with summer stock as
we know it today. We were the resident company, and we
played there from September through the following May. We
learned a new play every week, rehearsed every day, and
played every night except on Sunday. We also did three mati-
nees a week—learned our lines and got our wardrobes together in whatever time was left. We supplied our own
clothes. The players with the best and most varied wardrobes
were the most desirable ones to have in a company. I was paid
fifty dollars a week, and when we closed in June I had saved

the incredible amount of three hundred dollars with which to go back to New York. How on earth did I do it?

The company consisted of a leading man, a leading woman, a character man, a character woman, second man and second woman, juvenile and ingenue, and two or three others to fill in with "general business." We all lived in boardinghouses except the leading lady, who soon married the manager and went to live in a hotel.

I arrived with all the clothes I could get together. A white dress was most useful. First, it could be varied with different colored sashes. Then, the dress could be dyed, first a pastel color, and eventually, if it held together long enough, could be dyed brown or black. Large ostrich feather fans were also exceptionally useful (I had three of different colors) to dress up evening clothes in those Rachel Crothers flaming-youth type of plays that were so popular. We discovered a thrift shop run by the Episcopal Church where we could buy costumes very cheaply. They were the discarded clothes donated by rich people from Boston. It was fun to rummage among things and sometimes come up with a treasure that was almost brand-new and that fitted one perfectly. When we were on the stage and flattered by footlights and makeup we were very elegant indeed.

Each Saturday night when we were given our "sides" for the next week, we would first heft them in our hands to see if we had a long or a short part and then quickly check to see how many changes of costume there were. If one were to cut a manuscript horizontally in half one would arrive at about the size of our "sides." Sides had a paper covering with the name of the play, and inside were the lines for only one actor, with the three-word cue which led into the speech. The cue was often something as unenlightening as "so he says," or "oh yes, indeed." We waited until the first rehearsal on Tuesday to find out what the play was about. With the coming of copying machines and Xerox, actors can now have a manuscript to study, but for a long time manuscripts were an unknown luxury.

We studied our lines at every opportunity and put the sides

under our pillows at night in the hope that we would absorb some dialogue while we slept. Perhaps we did.

New Bedford adopted us. We were the town pets—"Our wonderful New Bedford Players." We were reviewed in the weekly newspaper and we had our fan clubs, usually made up of the factory girls. They would pick out one special performer for their affection and loyalty—usually it was the leading man or the leading woman or the juvenile. But I had my own fan club too. The girls came in a group every Saturday matinee and followed me home, walking at a respectful distance. They brought me presents of homemade fudge or hand-crocheted breakfast caps or camisoles.

Our dressing rooms were in the basement and after heavy rains there was so much water on the floor that we walked on planks to get in or out. The rooms had flimsy partitions about six feet high. Each dressing room contained a narrow makeup shelf with an electric bulb on either side of the mirror, two chairs, and the ever-present trunk that always smelled of greasepaint.

Theoretically, we were supposed to see the scenery and the hand props on the afternoon of the Monday-night performance, but sometimes we never saw the set until we actually stepped out before our opening-night audience. We would stick our parts in the back of one of the flats nearest our exit and would take a quick look between scenes.

At the end of the long season there were closing-night festivities with flowers and speeches and a party, and we took snapshots of each other and swore we would all meet again in Broadway plays.

Then came summer stock—and Lakewood. My heart glows whenever I think of it. One of the men in the New Bedford company had played there a year before, and I got the job of doing ingenue leads on his recommendation. The theatre was an old frame building set down among scattered cottages in a grove of trees on the shores of a beautiful lake. It was about five miles from Skowhegan, Maine, and was connected to the town by a little trolley car that rattled its way through the lovely countryside, carrying people who didn't have cars and who came to this summer resort to picnic, to swim, to fish, to canoe, to dance, or to go to the theatre.

Nothing could possibly have fulfilled my wants and wishes as Lakewood did. Here was a chance to spend the summer in an idyllic spot (my love for woods and water was rightfully inherited from New England forebears), but, more importantly, here was a chance to watch fine actors work and to learn as much as I could from them. It was a step up from New Bedford because the Lakewood company attracted some of the elite of Broadway. It attracted them because it was a perfect place to spend the summer and because the work was comparatively easy—only one matinee a week; also, it was a large company and everyone got an occasional week off. One thing actors did not come for was money. We were all paid exactly the same—thirty dollars a week and our room and board. The salary was no hardship as there was little to spend money for. We had free use of the canoes and boats, and about all we ever thought of buying was an occasional soft drink or a candy bar or hot buttered popcorn from the little store just outside the theatre. Fortunately, I did not have to worry about wardrobe, being well supplied with clothes from the long season in New Bedford. The whole place had a distinctly holiday atmosphere. We lived in summer cabins and had our meals at a long table in the community cottage.

On Saturday nights the movable chairs in the theatre were pushed back against the wall and there was a dance. Even though we worked hard learning parts, rehearsing and giving performances, somehow everyone found time for fishing or canoeing or swimming or golf or horseback riding. Sometimes we just walked in the woods and cued each other for next week's play. I remember with delight a certain morning when four of us got up two hours early and rode horseback to a field where we picked wild strawberries for breakfast. We liked each other and we had grand fun. In the seven summers that I played in Lakewood I made friendships that have lasted a lifetime.

Albert Hackett was the juvenile man—he remains a treasured friend—who later married Frances Goodrich, and they went to California where as a team they wrote some of the best pictures ever to come out of Hollywood. They came back to New York and collaborated on a play that won the Pulitzer Prize. It was the heartbreakingly beautiful *The Diary of Anne Frank*.

There was young Dick Halliday who would one day marry lovely Mary Martin and live happily ever after. There were Roy Bryant and Nila Mack who had once been the vaudeville team of Bryant and Mack—two of my dearest friends—and there were handsome Jean Dixon and blessed Jean Adair. There were the playwright John B. Hymer and his adorable wife, Elinore. They owned a house in Lakewood and came there every summer. We were always welcomed, and it was a favorite place for us to gather around the old upright piano and sing. (One of our songs was "You're Not the Type," which Bryant and Mack had set to music.) The Hymers often had guests from the Broadway theatre world and they always brought them to see our shows. Al Lewis, of the Lewis and Gordon producing firm, was a frequent visitor. Arthur Byron and his family were there, and Don Marquis came to act the lead in his own play, *The Old Soak*. Occasionally, a new play was tried out there.

Coming back to New York to look for work again was a letdown, but I was full of hopes and dreams and now I had some friends. I lived in a series of cheap rooms those winters in New York. Once it was an alcove that had been made into a bedroom by means of closing the sliding double doors that led to a living room where violin lessons were given all day. I didn't mind it much as I was almost always out hunting for that job that never materialized.

And then I found "my room"—the first room I had lived in that was not a bedroom. It was in a once elegant but now shabby railroad flat in an old apartment building on Broadway and 71st Street. It cost twelve dollars a week and was well worth that extravagant sum. It had a pull-out sofa bed which made it into a little living room in the daytime. It had a desk, a small table, and a comfortable chair. Its dormer window looked down on Broadway which to me was the most beautiful view in the world. And when I had covered my square trunk with a piece of chintz, shoved it under the window and furnished it with two pillows, it made a window seat. There was a bathroom at the end of the hall, and I had "kitchen privileges" which meant that I could get my own breakfast. I was ecstatic! Here was home at last!

In the meanwhile, Dick Halliday had sent "You're Not the Type" to *Liberty* magazine. It was not only published but they sent me a check for fifteen dollars. I squandered the whole amount on things to make the room really mine. I bought two Jessie Rittenhouse anthologies of poetry with smooth bright red-leather covers (that was where I first met Edna St. Vincent Millay). I bought a quilt patterned with bright red roses. This was put out of sight in the daytime but was lovely to snuggle under at night. And I bought a tea set for five dollars in Macy's basement. It was now a living room and it was mine—all mine. I was radiantly happy. I got out my mandolin, set my typewriter on the desk, and wrote a verse about it all. The little poem was bought by *McCall's* magazine and published with a small drawing of a dormer window at the top. Here it is:

MY ROOM

> My little room it is so small
> You might not think it fine at all.
> But it is home because you see
> It holds my trunk, my dreams, and me.
> A cretonne couch with cushions bright
> That turns into a bed at night,
> Desk, table, tea set, easy chair
> And softly shaded lamps are there;
> And when a friend drops in for tea
> We are as merry as can be;
> And cozy from the window seat
> I look down on a busy street.
> Sometimes adventure beckons there
> But when I see the pain and care,
> The disillusionment and doubt,
> My rosy curtains shut it out.

There is no place for gloom within—
My friends, my books, my mandolin.
My little room is up so high
Its window holds a starry sky
And here among the cushions curled
Night gives to me a jeweled world.
'Tis then my fancies love to stray
And little dreams come out to play—
Dreams that are gay and wistful too.
My room is one of them come true.

No jobs all winter, but it was wonderful to have Lakewood to look forward to. I took the State of Maine Express in May, went to sleep to the lovely clack-clacking of railroad ties, and woke up to the good smell of Maine in the morning.

Al Lewis was again a summer visitor at the Hymers' home. By this time he had seen me play a number of parts and had decided that I was the right actress to follow June Walker in one of the Lewis and Gordon productions called *The Nervous Wreck* when it went on tour in the autumn. He gave me a contract for it then and there.

I was in seventh heaven. I came down to earth only long enough to sign my name. Here at last was a leading part in a hit play under one of the best managements in New York. Here, after three years of desperate searching, was what I had been praying for—a chance to do something really first class, a chance to follow a Broadway star in the road company of a Broadway success. I was jubilant beyond words. The summer went by on wings. I had never been happier.

Back in New York I put on my best dress and floated on a pink cloud all the way to the Lewis and Gordon office to meet that famous playwright Owen Davis. He was not only the author of *The Nervous Wreck* but of so many other successes that he was one of the most important men on the Broadway scene. I was ushered into the private office and introduced to this massive man. He was so large he seemed to fill the room. He took one look at me and said I was not the type and he didn't want me in his play. The fact that I had a signed contract meant only that they would pay me two weeks' salary in lieu of two weeks' notice, and at seventy-five dollars a week that was no great consideration.

I was stunned and heartbroken. I was not so much as allowed to read the part. I had lost my first good job before I even had it. They told me I could play the small part of the ingenue which I indignantly refused. I had been engaged for the lead. Well, they told me, I could understudy whomever they got to play "my part." In tears, I stumbled blindly into the outer office. A thin young man in horn-rimmed glasses was standing there. Someone, probably Max Gordon, said, "Dorothy Stickney, this is Howard Lindsay. He writes some of our vaudeville acts." The young man couldn't help seeing that I was in desperate trouble. He offered to take me to lunch. I told him of my tragedy—how I had been fired without even being given a rehearsal.

This scholarly-looking Mr. Lindsay (whom I was not to meet again until the next spring) gave me some good advice. He said, "You have found yourself in a bad situation. The best thing you can do is to behave so well that it will put Lewis and Gordon under an obligation to you so they will give you the next good part that comes along." Did I take this advice? Not at all! I screamed my head off to anyone who would listen and to a lot of people who didn't want to listen. I pursued poor Owen Davis backstage relentlessly until he must have dreaded the sight of me. "How do you *know* I'm not right for the part when you won't give me a rehearsal?" But I settled for understudying Kathleen Comeges whom they engaged to play the lead. It was humiliating business—but it was a job. We went on the road. Otto Kruger who played the other lead was a fine actor, and I learned a lot from watching him. Naturally, I thought Kathleen Comeges was terrible. If ever I got a chance to go on—I would show them! I would show them all what a mistake they had made. I lived on this comforting fantasy. In February Kathleen Comeges decided to leave. Someone must have said—why not let the Stickney girl take over and get her out of our hair? So I was engaged to open in Providence on a Monday night. My big chance at last.

That day my monthly period arrived and as always made

me very sick. Otto Kruger, seeing how tense and scared I was, gave me a teaspoonful of brandy. It only made me sicker. My dressing room was in the basement, it had no windows, and there were heating pipes running across the ceiling. I stepped out on the stage to prove myself and, figuratively speaking, fell flat on my face. I was terrible. My voice failed and I could not be heard beyond the third row. I was fired again that night.

I wasn't even good enough to keep on being an understudy. As an actress I was finished. I told myself, bitterly, that I had never been any good and had wasted four years trying. I wasn't accustomed to crying but back in my hotel room the dam burst and I cried so hard and so loudly that a man from the next room telephoned to ask if he could be of some help. I cried more quietly after that. I was through. I considered jumping out the window. I opened it and quickly closed it and backed away. When I returned to New York the next night, it was darker inside me than it was outside the train windows.

There seemed to be no one to advise me what to do now, so I went to Evangeline Adams, the popular astrologer. Should I marry the boy from Dickinson who had once asked me? Should I try to write? Should I give up all idea of acting? Evangeline Adams took down my birth date and read my chart. She told me not to consider giving up acting until after January first of the next year. (Her advice was uncannily right.) At least there was Lakewood to look forward to. That summer things were to happen that would change my life.

In the spring Howard Lindsay was engaged to direct at Lakewood. He was told that he could have a free hand in choosing his cast—with one exception. The ingenue had played there for the past two summers and the management wanted her back again. Her name was Dorothy Stickney and would Mr. Lindsay please meet her. He was given my phone number and once more he invited me to lunch. I told him I wanted experience and would like to play all the longest parts. He was somewhat taken aback. Here was a brash little girl who seemed to be taking a lot for granted. He couldn't have liked me very much, and I don't blame him.

That turned out to be the perfect summer. Howard was a fine director and I was eager to learn. He was the first person who actually taught me about this thing called "technique." Instead of stumbling around, depending upon inspiration and hoping for the best, I was beginning to learn *how* it was done. In Howard's words: "Acting is to mean what you say sincerely in order to tell the audience exactly what you mean. Everything that is done on the stage must be seen, heard, and understood. That is technique. An actor doesn't learn to act until he is in front of an audience." He taught me that there were definite ways of making a point—of giving importance to a certain scene. Decide which is the important word in a line, or the important line in a speech, or the important scene in a play. Protect it by doing specific things. If you want the audience's attention to a particular word either drop it in tone or raise it in tone to set it apart. Take a pause before an important line. Take a breath and a tiny pause before a word you want to emphasize. Know *how* a thing is done and be able to repeat it exactly—that is also technique. Howard always expressed himself clearly and understandably in direction. Once when I was playing a love scene badly he directed me, "Be starry-eyed." I knew what he meant. Sometimes, if I was giving a down performance he would say, "Star yourself." I knew what he wanted. It was heaven to be learning about my business. There were "tricks of the trade" and these were all things I wanted to know.

Howard acted as well as directed. It was a delight to both of us when we played together. We were beginning to be very necessary to each other. In midseason we played *Outward Bound*. We were the "halfways," the pathetic young couple who had committed suicide on earth and who drifted through the play clinging to each other. We found we were clinging to each other offstage as well as on. We had fallen gloriously, beautifully, confidently, irrevocably in love.

One midnight on our way back from the theatre, we sat on a bench in the arbor at the edge of the lake. The soft night was cloudy and luminous, with a moon hidden somewhere in the mist and beyond the clouds. A black lace tree was silhouetted against the silver of lake and sky. It was so still we could hear the ripples break. A bird sang once. The air smelled of phlox and the earth was full of wonder. We knew we were bound joyously to each other for the rest of our lives. When we finally said good night, I stood for a long time alone on the porch just looking out at the lake, so lost in the glory that I dared not move lest I break the spell.

How to describe what it was like to be young and in love and full of the future? How to describe the joy of just being alive? We laughed a lot. We walked in the woods a lot. And we sang a lot. "When Day Is Done" and "What Is This Thing Called Love?" were new then. We played games about what it would be like to be very old together. We talked endlessly about the theatre. We canoed at night, sometimes sliding noiselessly under the branches of overhanging trees while Howard smoked his cigarette, making a tiny red hole in the dark.

One night, coming back from the theatre, we threw our flashlight into the lake to see how long it would stay lighted. Then we sat on the end of the pier with our feet dangling and watched the little fishes swim around this strange object and bump their noses against the light. That was a superior flashlight. It stayed lighted until almost dawn. When it went out we said our overdue good night and went to our separate beds.

The young man who had been the army officer I was so romantic about that long-ago June was back from South America. He journeyed to Lakewood to see me and brought a vicuna rug and a five-pound box of candy. I was too much in love with Howard to be more than polite, and, I hope, properly grateful for his gifts. I was glad when he left and I had no more distractions.

Even if I had not been in love with Howard Lindsay I would have recognized what a very special person he was and would have admired him. I don't rightly know how to put him into words. It is as difficult as if I tried to describe myself. I can put down facts, but the personality, the character, the quality of the man do not seem to be covered by facts.

He was of medium height, rather slight of build. He had light brown hair and gray eyes, and he wore horn-rimmed glasses. He had a kind of dignity and reserve that sometimes kept people at a distance. Actors who have worked under his direction say that they used to be afraid of him until they really knew him. He had a twinkle in his eyes and a lovely sense of the ridiculous. He was a master of the anticlimax as a comedy device and was immensely amused by it. He had no sense of the importance of money. It was something to be used, not hoarded. This was one of the many things we had in common. He was a "soft touch." If he knew that someone was down on his luck he didn't wait to be asked, but would volunteer, "Don't you need some dough?" This disregard for money was remarkable, considering his background. He had grown up in real poverty but it had left no scars on him. His childhood was spent in Atlantic City with his grandmother and his mother who had moved there with her four children after divorcing his father. She had been given a job as compositor on her brother's newspaper the Atlantic City *Union*. Her salary was ten dollars a week and this plus his grandmother's small army pension somehow supported the family.

Howard was the youngest, and since his mother was away working most of the time it was his grandmother who brought him up and whom he adored. Howard sold his uncle's newspapers on the Boardwalk, yelling at the top of his voice, "Daily *Union* one cent, to help my mother pay the rent." I have a photograph of him with newspapers under his arm. He looks to be no more than five years old. Could he possibly have been that young? He is wearing a small cap, a blouse with a floppy tie, his knee pants are too big for him, and so are his badly scuffed shoes.

Here are his own words from the book called *Five Boyhoods*, which he shares with Harry Golden, Walt Kelly, John Updike, and William K. Zinsser. He wrote: ". . . I became an actor on a 'due bill.' Since we were my uncle's poor relations, when advertisers in his paper couldn't pay their bills we were allowed to take it out in trade. One I recall was a photographer who couldn't pay his bill and we all had our pictures taken. And a teacher of elocution came to Atlantic City and advertised for pupils. She didn't pay her bill, either. I was sent to work it out. I went to her little cubbyhole on the Board-walk twice a week, from the age of four to the age of eight, and learned to recite hundreds of pieces. Any time there was an occasion where people were gathered together, I recited. Any time two or more people were in the same room with me they were in danger. The Boardwalk, of course, gave access to the summer hotels. They were wooden frame buildings with porches and porch chairs. So I would go along the verandas trying to sell my papers. When there was a group of people sitting together I would approach, take off my cap, and launch into a piece. At the end of this I would pass my cap. I was given some pennies and nickels and occasionally a dime. I remember clearly one day when I was fortunate enough to bring home over a dollar. This was very useful to my family. . . ."

When Howard was twelve they moved to Dorchester, Massachusetts, where his mother had gotten a job working in a friend's drygoods store. After graduating from grammar school there, he was admitted to the Boston Latin School—a fine, highly respected institution which had been founded in 1635—where students were prepared to enter college. He loved those four years. Rose Fitzgerald and Joseph Kennedy were also students there, but they were rich Boston Irish and he didn't mix with them socially. He loved writing compositions, and on graduation he won second prize for declamation and scholarship which gave him one year at Harvard. He paid his room rent there by tending furnaces.

A catalogue of the American Academy of Dramatic Arts fell into his hands. He learned that the course was two semesters of six months each. After the first course one could go on the stage. Many did, so the catalogue claimed. It was his grandmother who found the money to pay his tuition and enough to live on while he studied for six months in New York. Back in Boston he got a job as an extra in a stock company for three dollars a week. In the fall he returned to New York and joined a touring company of *Polly of the Circus*. He played two parts and was stage manager. They did forty-two weeks of one-night stands. That must have been murderously hard work but he loved it. For his first few years in the theatre he earned a meager living, and for the next few years, to quote him, "My earning power fell below the standard of being meager." He had various makeshift jobs, tried the movies, worked in tent shows, and one season went on the road armed with a pointer to lecture while kinescope slides of geographical points of interest were shown on a screen. Sometimes, in slack periods, he typed menus for his meals.

Eventually, he had the good fortune to be taken into Margaret Anglin's Shakespearean company, first as an extra and then to play bits, and to be assistant stage manager. From that he went on to being her stage manager and, eventually, her director.

All this time he was trying to write plays. His first play to be produced on Broadway was in 1927, the same year we were married. It was also the year I got my first Broadway part, but more of that later.

In that glorious summer of 1926, two plays came my way. One was the tryout of a play called *The Squall*, and one was a manuscript of a play called *Chicago*, which I got my hands on by borrowing it from Hortense Alden, who was in Lakewood for the tryout and who was also being considered for a part in *Chicago*. I sat up all night reading it. There was a part that I desperately wanted to play. By this time I had had considerable experience playing eccentric characters, and I much preferred them to pretty ingenues.

Chicago was a satire on the justice system for murderesses if they happened to be young and good-looking. The part I wanted was Crazy Liz, a demented, old scrubwoman in jail among the beautiful and stylish. She was a religious fanatic who had committed a murder and who raved and ranted about her guilt, much to the annoyance of the other prisoners. She sang Salvation Army hymns and scrubbed out the jail cells— and occasionally let out a piercing scream for no reason except that she was crazy. She wore a dirty apron and the edges of her grubby long underwear showed below her sleeves. I knew I could play her. I was certainly going to try to get that part even though I knew my chances were slim.

For the Lakewood tryout of *The Squall*, Blanche Yurka and Pedro de Cordoba and Hortense Alden had been brought from New York for the star parts. Al Hackett and I filled in as juvenile and ingenue. The play—a melodrama laid in Spain—was to be done that autumn on Broadway. Blanche Yurka was the good wife, Pedro de Cordoba was the good husband, and Hortense Alden was the bad but beautiful little gypsy who spoke pidgin English and almost wrecked the good home. The play has long since been forgotten, but people remember critic Robert Benchley's review of it. At the end of the second act the little gypsy girl says: "Nuby, she good girl. Nuby, she stay here." Benchley wrote: "Benchley, he bad boy. Benchley, he go home."

At the end of the Lakewood season Howard and I went to Vermont to be with my father, who was there for a visit. It was the only time they were ever to see each other. We had one idyllic walk following the brook upstream two miles through the woods to Nineveh where my grandparents once had a farm. Nothing was left of it now except the cellar hole and a little of the foundation, the lilac bushes and a great clump of golden glow. We threw one of its yellow blossoms into the clear stream and followed its progress all the way down the hill to Tyson. We met some boys who had found a bee tree and they gave us a large chunk of honey in the comb, which we put between two enormous leaves to carry back.

On returning to New York the first thing I did was to go to Al Lewis and wangle a promise from him that they would let me at least read the part of Crazy Liz when they started auditioning the cast of *Chicago*. Lewis and Gordon had a large financial interest in that play, which Sam Harris was producing for his friend Jeanne Eagels.

In the meantime, my first Broadway part happened. *The Squall* was in rehearsal and the director was disappointed in the movie starlet they had gotten for the ingenue, so they offered the part to me. I was delighted to repeat what I had played when *The Squall* was tried out in Maine. The fact that it was only ten days before the opening didn't worry me in the least. I was accustomed to getting up in much longer parts in a much shorter time. They costumed me in bright pink ruffles and a little flowered Spanish shawl. Romney Brent was the juvenile. The night of the opening I took a taxi—an unthinkable luxury—down through Central Park on the way to the theatre. I felt very much the Broadway actress and very grand indeed. It was the only time in all my years in the theatre that I wasn't the least bit frightened or nervous facing an opening night. The play turned out to be a great success.

I had played in it happily for two weeks when a newspaper announced that *Chicago* was in rehearsal. Pretty ingenues didn't interest me nearly as much as eccentric characters, and I wanted beyond anything to play Crazy Liz. Maybe it wasn't too late.

I got out the stock wardrobe trunk and costumed myself in the dreariest, shabbiest clothes I could find. I skinned my hair back and wore no makeup except for some dark smudges on my cheeks and a few lines around my eyes to make me look older. Then, I tried to see Sam Harris. I went persistently every day for a week, armed with my character photographs and looking my worst—but I never got past the office boy. Then, one day as I was leaving dejectedly, I caught up with Sam Harris in the corridor waiting for the same elevator that I was about to take. I told him that Mr. Lewis had promised that I could read the part. I told him I was in *The Squall* and had just found out that *Chicago* was in rehearsal. He said, "Don't be silly, kid. You're in a hit. You're lucky. Stay there. You're too young for the part anyway, and, besides, we have already engaged a woman to play Liz." I begged him, "Please, Mr. Harris, could I just go and watch a rehearsal?" He said he didn't like people sitting out front, but he finally gave me a grudging consent. "All right. Go in the front entrance and sit down in back where no one can see you." I flew to the Music Box Theatre, crept in and sat down in the last row. Then the miracle happened. Mr. Harris came in the stage door and onto the stage. Sam Forrest, who was directing the play, greeted him, saying, "We can't go any further with this scene. The woman you sent for Crazy Liz didn't show up." I couldn't hear what they were saying after that, but I could see Mr. Harris' head nod in my direction. He came down to me and said, "If you want to read the part, go some place where there's light and look it over. Then you can try it." He handed me the sides and I went to the nearest place I could find where there was any light. It was in the gents' toilet on the balcony floor. The part was only fifteen sides long, but before I had read halfway through, someone yelled for me to come down. I knew how I wanted to do that part and, right or wrong, I played it for all I was worth. I didn't give a rehearsal. I gave a performance. When it said, "scream," I let out a maniacal yell. This was the part I had dreamed of acting. When the first scene was over everything stopped. Sam Harris came to me and said, "When can you give in your notice to *The Squall?*" I replied instantly: "Tonight." He told me to come to his office the next day, and he signed me to a three-year contract. So much for the long arm of coincidence that has been so much a part of my life.

Jeanne Eagels consented to have me play the part only if I wore a black wig. Even though I was a bedraggled old scrubwoman, she would have no other blond in the cast—so I was fitted for the black wig. The show was booked to open in Atlantic City before Christmas. The New York opening would be just before the New Year.

On my second day of rehearsing with the company, I witnessed something that heretofore I had only read of in bad fiction. Jeanne Eagels got angry with the director—I never did know what about—she threw the script down in the middle of the stage, screamed at Sam Forrest and called him every vile name in the book. She had the face of an angel and it was incongruous to hear those words coming out of that beautiful face. When her tantrum was over she walked out of the theatre and disappeared. Rehearsals were postponed for two weeks while Sam Harris frantically searched for her. She sent no word and no one could find out where she was hiding. One week before we were due to open out of town, Francine Larrimore was engaged for the part.

Howard came to Atlantic City to spend Christmas with me. That was where we had our first Christmas tree. It was not a large tree, but my hotel room was so small that we had to put it in the bathtub. Just the same, we had our tree, the first of many in years to come.

We opened in New York December 30—day after tomorrow it would be 1927—and I remembered the prediction of Evangeline Adams, the astrologer I had consulted. She had told me not to consider giving up the stage until the year 1927. The play was an instantaneous hit. It was the first of its genre to be seen on Broadway, cynical and terribly funny. After that came *Gentlemen of the Press*, *The Front Page*, and the like. But *Chicago* was the first. Sam Forrest had bowed out, and a lanky young man took over the direction. It was his first job of directing. His name was George Abbott.

On opening night I was halfway up the stairs to my dressing room when I came back down to see why the audience was applauding. The applause was for me. Crazy Liz was a hit too. The reviews were raves and I came in for a large share of praise from the critics.

When Howard's friends at The Players Club asked him about the girl he was engaged to, he delighted in telling them she was playing Crazy Liz in *Chicago*—and watching their startled reaction as they remembered the screaming hag, and tried to be polite and congratulate him.

Howard had written a play in collaboration with Bertrand Robinson who had been writing vaudeville sketches at about the same time as Howard was writing them. They got together on a charming comedy called *Tommy*. *Tommy* was a boy in love with a girl whose parents liked him so much and were so eager for the match that it naturally turned the girl against him. The play revolved around Tommy's desperate efforts to make the parents hate him so he could win back his girl. It was bought for production by George C. Tyler who was well known as producer of a certain kind of play. His plays were mostly comedies. They were always clean. Helen Hayes was the ingenue lead in many of them.

Tommy opened in New York on January 10. Howard and I had arrived on Broadway almost simultaneously—within a few days of each other. This was a good omen. We planned to be married in June. Of course I could not see the opening of Howard's first play, because I was acting in *Chicago*, but naturally he was there, sitting in the balcony. All went well until the end of the first act. Then the curtain did not come down. The actors ad-libbed valiantly. Howard started to rush backstage. He got halfway down the alley and then decided it was silly to go back as the curtain must surely be down by now. He returned to the theatre. The curtain was still up. This time he did go backstage and discovered that something had gone wrong with the mechanism and no signal had been given to the stagehands who were happily playing poker in the basement. The actors had almost run out of ad-libs when the curtain finally descended.

In the second act a very important prop was left offstage. The actors covered as best they could. The prop wasn't found until the show was over. It had been safely locked away in the property trunk. That was the night that Howard made a vow never again to go to an opening of any play he wrote. It was a vow he kept to the end of his life.

Some friends gave us an opening-night party and we stayed until three o'clock when we could get the first edition of a morning paper. We stopped the taxi under a street light to read Alan Dale's review. He ended every paragraph with: ". . . and so on, ad nauseum." It was a terrible blow to say good night on. The next day the world looked rosier again for all the other papers gave *Tommy* good notices. The show was a success and had a respectably long run.

At one time during that winter we faced some horrid news. We could not be married in the Catholic Church because Howard had been married before. The marriage had lasted only two years and there had been a divorce some time before we ever met. According to church law a Catholic could not be married to a divorced person. I paced the floor all that night wondering what to do. In the eyes of the Church if I married Howard I could no longer be a Catholic. I would be excommunicated. I shudder to think that I was on the verge of missing the greatest thing that ever happened in my life. Then, a kindly priest came to our rescue. We both knew this priest and he really wanted to have us marry. The Church, when necessary, can bring into play a detective system that would put the FBI to shame. This wonderful priest instigated an investigation of old files and discovered—Lord knows how—that Virginia, Howard's ex-wife, had been baptized a Catholic. She had never practiced the Catholic religion and neither she nor Howard knew about the baptism. They had not been married by a priest; therefore, in the eyes of the Church the marriage had never existed; therefore, I was free to marry Howard and remain a Catholic. Now we must wait for the official letter confirming the permission for us to marry.

I wrote to Dad asking him if he could come East for our marriage. The letter crossed a letter from my sister telling me that Father was dying of cancer. Dad also wrote, insisting that things were under control and suggesting that I need not hurry home. I gave in my notice and left for Dickinson.

Being a doctor he had no illusions about what suffering lay ahead and what the end would be. He was unbelievably wonderful. He made no complaints, but quietly put his affairs in order and waited patiently for the ordeal to be over. He was excited and stimulated by Lindbergh's solo flight across the Atlantic. He talked about it with cheerful animation. His old friends came to see him and left in tears. I was with him when he died late in July.

On the day of the funeral the whole town closed; all the stores, all the business buildings shut their doors. There were crowds of people at the cemetery, not only people I knew but many who were strangers to me—cowboys and farmers and women with shawls over their heads had come to say goodbye to their beloved doctor.

A few days later I took the train back to New York and to Howard. We went immediately to Lakewood and waited impatiently for that official letter which would give us permission to have a Catholic wedding. In the early mail one morning the letter came. We wasted no time. We phoned the nearest priest for an appointment that day. He was in Waterville, a town five miles away. His parish was composed mostly of French Canadian factory workers who spoke little English. He seemed delighted at the prospect of marrying two theatre people from Lakewood.

I got out the best my wardrobe had to offer—a short-skirted flapper sort of dress of pink shantung. The dress was nothing special but I did have a beautiful wide-brimmed pink hat made of transparent straw. I got myself put together and we borrowed a Ford. On the road we picked up two actor friends and asked them to come and be our witnesses. We had no wedding ring, so we bought one in the Waterville Woolworth's on our way to the priest's house. It was a perfectly beautiful blue-and-gold day and we were happy beyond words, so we sang all the way over and all the way back— "Blue skies smiling on me—nothing but blue skies do I see." The month was August and the date was Friday the thirteenth. Bad-luck symbols have always been good luck for Howard and me. If a black cat refuses to cross our path, we cross its.

The ceremony took place in the little front parlor of the parish house. It had lace antimacassars and a rubber plant. The priest sat us all down and gave us an interminable lecture on the Holy Roman Church, not leaving out anything. He particularly relished the part about the defection of Henry VIII. I was the only Catholic in the party and he did his best to convert the other three. We all sat with our eyes cast down, not daring to look at each other for fear we would laugh. Finally he said reluctantly, "The service itself is very short." Then he opened the book and read those most beautiful of all words in the English language—"From this day forward to have and to hold, to love and to cherish, for better or worse, for richer,

for poorer, in sickness and in health, till death do us part."
And we were married.

———————

This is a piece that Howard wrote for the *Saturday Review*:

We had been married for six months before my wife
and my mother met. The first confrontation had its
surprises as well as its difficulties. The first surprise came
to my mother. She knew I had married an actress. I am
sure she had imagined her to be somewhat like the lush fe-
male on the poster of "The Girl from Rector's." She was
not prepared for that wide-eyed chit of a child stretched
out on the couch, her pale forehead contracted in pain. I
explained to mother that Dorothy was not well. She had a
severe headache. All her life mother had been subject to
what were then called "sick headaches" and she was instantly sympathetic. What we could not tell mother was
that Dorothy was suffering from her first hangover.

The night before, Dorothy and I had been down in the
Village at a party. It was given by one of the gayest and
most charming couples in New York, Miriam Hopkins
and Bill Parker. We drank more than our wont. At that
time Dorothy hadn't cultivated any wont and knew nothing of the consequences of drinking too much. We had
talked and laughed and sung and at six in the morning
Miriam cooked us some breakfast. There just aren't any
parties like that any more, unless they are being given by
people who are as young now as we were then. That
Dorothy was to meet her mother-in-law the next day
seemed unimportant.

Mother was a small, delicate-looking woman, a wisp of
New England granite. We had a part-time maid, which I
knew struck mother as an extravagance, but she held her
peace. I had ordered a simple and frugal dinner which

mother seemed to enjoy. Dorothy sat with us at the table, ate little, and contributed less to the conversation. After the coffee had been served, mother held Dorothy's eye and asked, "What do you do with your old coffee grounds?" The throb in Dorothy's temple jumped into high gear. Had my wife been in perfect health and high spirits, I submit this was an unfair question. "I don't know what we do with them," she stammered, looking very guilty. "I guess we just throw them away." "You can use them for flavoring," mother said smugly. "Make your own coffee jello."

I, too, had been bewildered by mother's question, but now I knew that mother had accepted our marriage and was trying to contribute to it.

The first night of our marriage we spent in Howard's cottage. On Saturday morning there was a telegram informing me that I was to report for rehearsal on Tuesday. Before I had left *Chicago* I had contracted to go back into the cast when the road tour started. I said good-bye to Howard and took a train for New York. Howard went fishing. That was our honeymoon.

We rehearsed two weeks as there were new people in the cast; then we opened in Chicago. Howard joined me there and stayed until the run was over, then we both went back to New York.

We found a little duplex apartment on West Tenth Street which was exactly right. It had a small kitchen, a living room with a fireplace, and french doors opening onto a good-sized terrace. The bedroom and bath were directly above and connected to the living room by a tiny narrow stairway. The terrace overlooked the lovely back gardens of the houses on Eleventh Street. We put a white picket fence around the terrace and planted garden boxes with petunias.

The next spring I got the part of Claudia Kitts in a revival of *March Hares.* Richard Byrd, Josephine Hull, and Genevieve Tobin were in the cast. This was another character part and the most complete contrast to Crazy Liz imaginable. It was a comedy baby-ingenue who wore beautiful clothes and a pretty makeup. I loved playing her. The play only lasted a few weeks, but I had come off well with the critics.

In August another character part came my way. I was cast as Molly Malloy—"a Clark Street tart"—in *The Front Page.* I broke my elbow at the dress rehearsal the night before the New York opening and was so excited that I didn't even know it until three days later. Molly Malloy was a short part and a good one. Her first scene takes place in the pressroom high up in the Criminal Courts Building in Chicago. Reporters are sitting around playing poker. They are awaiting the early morning execution of a man named Earl Williams who has been found guilty of murder. Molly Malloy, a pathetic little streetwalker, storms onto the stage in a fury. Her opening line is: "I have been looking for you bastards!"

A lot of kidding goes on among the reporters. Here are cut versions of Molly's two scenes.

ENDICOTT: Say, Molly, those were pretty roses you sent Earl Williams. What does he want done with them tomorrow morning?

MOLLY: You cheap crumbs been making a fool out of me long enough . . . I never said I loved Earl Williams and was willing to marry him on the gallows. You made that up—and all that other bunk about my being his soulmate and having a love nest with him.

MCCUE: Well, didn't you?

ENDICOTT: You've been sucking around that cuckoo ever since he has been in the death house. Everybody knows you're his affinity.

MOLLY: That's a lie! I met Mr. Williams just once in my life, when he was wandering around in the rain without his hat or coat on—like a sick dog—the day before the shooting, and I went up to him like any human being would and I asked him what was the matter. And he told me about being fired after working at the same place twenty-two years. And I brought him up to my room because it was warm there.

ENDICOTT: Did he have the two dollars?

MURPHY: Aw—put it on a Victrola record.

MOLLY: I tell you he just sat there talking to me all night. He just sat there talking and never once laid a hand on me. And in the morning he went away and I never seen him again till the day of the trial.

ENDICOTT: Why didn't you adopt him instead of letting him run around shooting policemen?

SCHWARTZ: Suppose that cop had been your own brother?

MOLLY: I wish to God it had been one of you!

MURPHY: Say, what's the idea of this song and dance anyway? This is a pressroom. We're busy.

SCHWARTZ: Go on home.

(*They try to push her out the door.*)

MOLLY: Keep your dirty hands off me—you low-down heels—you dirty punks! (*She exits.*)

In the second scene she and Hildy Johnson (played by Lee Tracy) discover the prisoner, who has escaped. They hide him in a rolltop desk before the other reporters come swarming back to the pressroom. The reporters are suspicious, they converge on Molly, hurling questions at her.

WOODEN SHOES: Where is he?

MOLLY: Go find out—you lousy heels! You don't think I am going to tell?

WOODEN SHOES: You'll tell all right. We'll make you.

MURPHY: Come on, you lousy tart, before we kick your teeth in. (*They are closing in on her. She picks up a chair to ward them off and backs toward the window.*)

MOLLY: No you don't! You bastards! Keep away from me!

KRUGER: Grab her!

MOLLY: You'll never get it out of me! Never!

(*She leaps for the open window and disappears. Her scream of terror and exaltation is heard as she falls to the ground.*)

This was not a faked jump. It was real. A six-foot hole had been cut in the floor under the stage window, so instead of jumping and ducking, I actually went straight down to the basement, landing on a mattress. On dress rehearsal night, going down, I hit my elbow on the edge of the floor. But the air was so electric with excitement that I wasn't aware of its hurting much. However, three days later when I tried to pound on the pressroom door my right arm would not work. A doctor X-rayed it and told me I had broken a tip off the elbow bone. I played the next three weeks with my elbow in a cast and my arm in a black sling to match the sleazy black lace dress I was wearing. I found—thanks to the plaster cast—that I could still jump out the window without too much trouble. The audience didn't seem to notice, though they must have thought I had a peculiar mannerism of holding one arm stiffly.

Breaking my elbow was not important compared to a discovery I made one night. I discovered, with pleasurable surprise, that I had passed a milestone in my development as an actress. I suddenly knew what I was doing. I knew that I would be able to do the scene exactly the same way the next night and the next and the next. It was my first intimation that I really knew something dependable about the technique of acting. Then I got sick and had to be out of the play for four weeks.

Howard loved his club—The Players. All his life it had been extremely important to him. The Players is a most distinguished club, housed in a beautiful old building on Gramercy Park. It had once been the home of Edwin Booth. He had bequeathed it for a clubhouse to the men of his profession and men of the allied arts. Howard had become a member in 1917 when he was just back from the war. He was a devoted Player and took great pride in this elegant club so rich in tradition. In 1955, he was elected its president, as successor to Edwin Booth, Joseph Jefferson, John Drew, and Walter Hampden.

Every year The Players produced an all-star revival of a play for a limited engagement of only the first week in June. Those were the days when stars were not inevitably tied up to

Hollywood contracts and it was easy to get a star cast. I was not a star but they paid me the compliment of inviting me to be in *The Beaux Stratagem* which they had chosen for 1928. I played Cherry, the young serving maid. Howard was as proud and flattered as I was about having been included in this distinguished gathering.

After the closing on Saturday night a supper party was always given at the club in honor of the cast. It was a beautiful occasion about which the word "glamour" could truthfully be used. The dining room was filled with flowers and its doors were opened onto a garden, where the fountain played. The men were in dinner clothes and the women in their prettiest evening dresses (mine was of white chiffon with a red camellia at the neck). There were toasts to the ladies, and speeches and compliments and presents. That year the gifts were silver picture frames with our names and the dates engraved on them. It was an altogether glittery and gay affair.

Howard and I were among the last to leave, about three in the morning. We were still too happy and excited to go home to bed, so we took a taxi and drove around and around Central Park. There had been a little shower during the evening and the park was washed clean and fragrant. Then we had the driver take us to Times Square, which was very strange at that hour. It gave one an eerie feeling to see it so silent and deserted. By seven o'clock we dismissed the cab in front of Child's and went in to have breakfast and to read the Sunday *Times* which had nice things to say about the play.

In 1930, I got another fine character part to the play, only this time it was the lead. My first lead. I played the illiterate wife of a taxi driver, a real "deese, dem and dose" kind of part in a play called *The Up and Up*. I loved it. We went into rehearsal, and then I got sick again. It was acute colitis, an inability to eat and a terrible weakness. They had to open out of town with the understudy. Howard was directing the play and he himself supplied the money to keep it on the road an extra week while they waited for me to get better. I tried frantically to get well enough to work. I would *will* myself to get out of bed, but when I stood on my feet I would faint. I blamed myself for getting sick, but didn't know what to do about it. Neither did the doctors. I had the most awful sense of guilt for having let everybody down. The play opened in New York with the understudy. It closed in a week. I promised myself that I must never again disappoint myself and other people. *Never*. But I was frightened.

In the next two years Howard, in collaboration with Bert Robinson, had two plays on Broadway. They were *Your Uncle Dudley* and *Oh, Promise Me*. They were both moderately successful.

I had always wanted to be in a play by that fine playwright George Kelly who had given us *The Show-Off* and *The Torchbearers* and so many others. My chance came in December. It was a short part—another eccentric character—a half-mad poet called Miss Krail in *Philip Goes Forth*. The part was beautifully written and a joy to act. The play had a short run and deserved better.

The next year (1932) came my first really big part. Rose Franken had written a play called *Another Language*. Helen Hayes had turned it down and they got me for the part of Stella. This time it was not a character part but a straight lead. A star part, in fact. I longed to play her, but I was terrified of playing myself in front of an audience. Always before I had had a character to hide behind. I needed the heady sensation of being someone else, which had always before protected me. This time I would have to be myself. Stella was a young wife married into the very plebeian Hallem family. Glenn Anders was her husband. Margaret Wicherly was the matriarch of the Hallem clan. They didn't like Stella very much because she was so different from the rest of them. Figuratively, they spoke another language. John Beal was the Hallem grandson. He falls in love with Stella who, having married into the family, is now his aunt.

We went into rehearsal and I found that I simply didn't know how to play myself on the stage. I felt I was miserably bad. So bad indeed that I went to Arthur Beckhard who was director as well as producer to give in my notice. He refused to accept it—thank God, as things turned out. So I stumbled

As a Folies Bergere girl. I'm wearing my symmetricals (LEWIS SMITH)

As Crazy Liz in
Chicago (HAL PHYFE)

As Molly Molloy in *The
Front Page* (PHOTOGRAPH
BY VANDAMM)

With John Beal and Glenn Anders in *Another Language*
(PHOTOGRAPH BY VANDAMM)

As Granny in *On Borrowed Time*

Howard and me in front of our farmhouse in New Jersey
(PHOTO BY F. M. DEMAREST)

As Vinnie in *Life With Father* (PHOTOGRAPH BY VANDAMM)

Howard as Clare in *Life With Father* (PHOTOGRAPH BY VANDAMM)

To a new friend from
Dorothy Stickney and Howard Lindsay

One of our *Life With Father* families

Portrait by John Falker that hung in the lobby of the Empire Theatre

along as best I could. We opened in New York late in May, and to everyone's surprise we were the hit of the season. The critics were ecstatic about the play and more than kind to me. I had come out from behind those character parts with astonishing success. But after playing for two months, to my complete disgust I got sick again—another failure. It was the same old story. The same old colitis, the same old inability to eat, and the same old weariness. Doctors called it nervous exhaustion.

Nevertheless, I kept on playing. I could manage to eat enough oatmeal gruel to keep going, and at every performance a maid would stand in the wings with a Lily cup of champagne. At each exit I took a swallow which gave me enough vitality to get through the next scene. (To this day I hate champagne.) Finally, I had to give up altogether and go to bed. I lay motionless for what seemed a very long time. It was probably two or three weeks. Then I went back to finish the run of the play in New York, so thin that my clothes no longer fit. But thanks to a certain doctor I was able to go on the road with it. He remembered that in cases of diabetes, insulin gave one a false appetite—a sudden craving for food. And so, though I was not diabetic, he started giving me insulin about half an hour before meals. It had the desired effect. It worked. I was able to eat. The doctor taught me how to inject the insulin and eventually I was able to stick the needle in myself. I was glad to stop as soon as the road tour was over.

———

I had been very unhappy about my Catholicism since long before we were married. Howard had nothing to do with my questioning. He never tried to influence me in any way, but was the soul of goodness and patience during the two years it took me to make up my mind. I prayed a lot. I had discovered, for one thing, that I could not say the Apostles' Creed ("I believe these and all the truths which the Catholic Church believes and teaches . . .") and mean what I was saying, that I was professing to believe some things I definitely did not believe. It was an agonizing time. The turning point came one day in a doctor's waiting room. He was one of the doctors I had gone to trying to find out what was wrong with me, why I got sick so often. I had picked up a magazine and started reading a piece by that great preacher Harry Emerson Fosdick. In it he said that he had been talking to a young girl who was greatly troubled because she had just found out that God wasn't a Baptist. I laughed out loud, startling the other patients in the waiting room. It suddenly occurred to me that all along I had been thinking that God was a Catholic. Things were easier after that. I discovered the Emerson that I had taken from Father's library when my sister and I had divided the books after his death. Through Emerson I discovered the Bible and found it fascinating reading. Especially the beautiful poetry in the Old Testament. I read Emily Cady's *Lessons in Truth*. I read Judge Troward's lectures, and I read the Vedanta. I finally began to find a faith, a religion of my own which I believed in, and which helped me in daily life and in times of trouble.

The next spring we decided to go abroad. We couldn't afford it, but we went anyway. It would be a belated honeymoon. I had never been in Europe and Howard had been there only as a soldier stationed in France. He had organized the Brest Stock Company which he directed and acted in. He was doing his regular soldiering job and entertaining the troops besides.

A friend had told us about a little village in Austria with the improbable name of Igls. It was high in the Tyrol, just above Innsbruck. So high, in fact, that on some days the clouds were below us instead of above. It could be raining in Innsbruck while the sun was shining in Igls.

Dwight Wiman had commissioned Howard to dramatize a story by Edward Hope Coffey. The village of Igls turned out to be just the perfect place to write the play—sparkling and stimulating air and no interruptions. We lived in a small inn, and every morning after we had breakfasted on our little balcony overlooking the mountains, Howard would take his typewriter down to the summer house at the end of the garden and work for several hours. He wrote the whole play in eighteen days and it was very, very good—one of his best. It was called *She Loves Me Not*.

We spoke no German, except for a few useful phrases, and understood none, but the Austrians were warm and friendly and we smiled at each other a lot. Afternoons we would sometimes take the bus down the steep mountain to Innsbruck to visit a museum or an old castle, or to shop for music boxes or to buy a Lodenbauer coat or a dirndl. And we loved to watch squadrons of the small Austrian Army marching in the street with Alpine roses stuck in their bayonets—and looking for all the world like something straight out of a Shubert musical. We often just walked through the fields or in the woods, sometimes stopping at an inn to have beer and cheese in a vine-covered arbor. We were both very happy, in love with each other, and with Austria.

We eagerly looked forward to Midsummer Night, which was their Eve of St. John when the great fires would be lighted on all the mountains. It was a beautiful warm night and the air was full of fireflies. We joined the crowd that had come out to see the spectacle, then the bonfires began to be lighted. The first one outlined a huge heart and cross, the symbol of Austria, then the other fires began to blaze. They were all enormous swastikas on the mountains near and far, beautiful but somehow sinister. We knew little or nothing about Hitler or what was beginning to take shape in Germany; our peaceful village seemed untouched.

A letter of introduction to a family in Saxony had been given us by the man who imported the little painted music boxes which I loved so much and which were the start of my collection at home. They were made in all kinds of fantasies—little carved and painted figures that seemed to march around when the top revolved as the crank was turned. Our letter was to the Saxon family who made them.

We hired a car and an English-speaking driver. On the way to Saxony we would stop for a few days to see that Christmas town, that fairy-tale town, that toy town of Nuremberg. We looked forward to it with delight. When we crossed the German border we watched with surprise as the driver stopped and put a small flag with a swastika on the hood of the car. We were equally surprised when even small children greeted us as we passed with a raised right arm and one word shouted —"*Heil!*" In Nuremberg we were shocked, surprised, and dismayed. It was not the fairy-tale town we had envisaged. It was more like a Nazi camp. Every shop window showed a picture of Hitler and flew a swastika flag. The city was full of brown shirts and boots. They never walked—they marched. And when you saw a squadron of them coming you quickly got out of their way. We were truly frightened. We were shaken by the atmosphere of evil, and we couldn't get out fast enough. We told the driver we had changed our minds about Saxony and he was to drive us straight back to Austria. Not long after that we said good-bye to Igls and started for home. The day we left the head of the Austrian Government was killed. The Nazis had murdered Dollfuss.

When we came back to New York late in the summer of 1933 *She Loves Me Not* was quickly cast and put into rehearsal. The cast included John Beal, Burgess Meredith, and Philip Ober as Princeton students, and there was also a cute little chorus girl named Polly Walters. She had never had a speaking part before, and she was sent down to our apartment to have Howard look her over and see if she would do. He asked me to listen in from the top of the stairs in the bedroom above and tell him what I thought. I heard Howard ask her if she really wanted to be an actress, and heard her reply in a little high-pitched voice with a distinctly Bronx accent: "Oh yes, Mr. Lindsay. I don't think there's any future in adagio dancing." We both knew instantly that she was a natural—a perfect piece of typecasting for the part of Curley who is a little dancer in a second-rate nightclub. Curley is wanted by the police because she has witnessed a gangland murder that took place right in the middle of her solo number. She has run away and gone as far by bus as her money will take her. When she reaches Princeton she is out of cash. She looks in the window of a dormitory room and sees a young man eating a large piece of cake. Her hunger gets the best of her and she knocks on the door and tells him she is hungry. Two of the boys take her in and give her what is left of the cake. They are somewhat startled when she takes off her coat and they see she is dressed only in her spangled bra and very short pants. They decide to hide her from the police. They cut her hair short, dress her in boys' clothes, and hope to pass her off as a visiting cousin.

All sorts of complications follow. They involve not only the police but also the Communist Party, a motion-picture press agent, a gangland thug, the president of a bank, and even the dean of the college and his beautiful daughter. Raymond Sovey had designed a wonderfully ingenious stage set. It consisted of two fairly large stages, one above the other, in the center, the boys' bedrooms; and four smaller stages, also one above the other, on each side. These levels were used for scenes in the dean's office, the Communist headquarters, people on telephones, and so on. Blackouts were used throughout to speed up the action.

I was detailed, as usual, to go to the opening and report. Howard, as usual, went to The Players to play pool or bridge, until the evening was over. I was pretty nervous until the second and third big laughs came. Then, I knew we were in, and I did wish Howard had been there. It was his first smash hit on Broadway.

The critics were ecstatic. Brooks Atkinson wrote: "Nothing could convey the exuberance that roared out at the 46th Street Theatre. Last night's audience grew more and more helpless as this hair-brained comedy danced a leapfrog through imaginative absurdities. Staging a hurly-burly comedy as resourcefully as this involves tremendous technical skill. As his own director Mr. Lindsay has finished the job perfectly. 'She Loves Me Not' races through a blaring evening without stumbling for a minute—a roaring, romping junket of fun, spontaneous, guileless and tumultuous."

John Mason Brown wrote: "It forces you to check your common sense with your hat and compels you to laugh yourself blue in the face by the ceaseless invention of its writing, by the swift excellence of its production, and the rollicking spirit of its fooling."

Gilbert Gabriel wrote: "Last night's laughter was prairie wide and fire-engine loud. We were seeing the funniest show in years."

Howard was hailed by the press as Broadway's newest and most brilliant playwright and director. He was now the white-haired boy of the theatre. The play had a long run to sold-out houses.

Practically the same company was taken to London the next summer. The British simply did not understand why the Americans had found this show so funny and it soon closed.

Just before rehearsals started for the New York company, a young man named Joshua Logan telephoned Howard. Howard knew him only as a member of the University Players. They were a talented group who organized a summer theatre in Falmouth, and later their own stock company in Baltimore. In that company were Henry Fonda, Margaret Sullavan, Myron McCormick, Norris Houghton, Bretaigne Windust, and James Stewart. The company had been an artistic success but a financial failure. Josh was back in New York broke and looking for a job. He had exactly twenty-five cents left. He decided he would make five phone calls—they were only a nickel then—and if there was no work forthcoming from any of the calls he told himself he would give up the theatre and find some other way to make a living. Nothing resulted from the first four calls. With his last nickel he called Howard Lindsay. Howard told him he had nothing worthwhile, but if it was just work he wanted he could be assistant stage manager and general understudy at a small salary in *She Loves Me Not*. Josh accepted with alacrity. That was the start of his long and illustrious career in show business. I can remember sitting on a hard bench backstage and hearing him say, "Dorothy, do you think I could ever get to be a director?"

We had been married only a few years when the farmhouse and the apple tree happened. A young couple who were our close friends had found a Dutch colonial house in a sparsely settled part of New Jersey. They wanted us to have one too. Howard was writing plays and I was acting at every opportunity. We loved our little two-room apartment and we loved New York. If there was anything in the world we did not want it was the country. But when our friends, bursting with enthusiasm, said they had found the perfect house for us (very cheap), we agreed between ourselves that out of politeness we would have to at least look at the thing, after which we would say a quick "no" and catch the first train back to New York.

We went on a February day that was bleak with sleet and mud. The house looked small and lonely in that stark countryside. It was built into the side of a hill, was made of fieldstone, and looked as though it had been there forever. First we sloshed our way around the outside and discovered chiseled into the cornerstone the astonishing date of 1741. It had been there forever. The room on the lowest level was a drab kitchen with broken linoleum on the floor and a stove in the middle. The chimney stuck through the clapboard wall into what had to be a fireplace because we had noticed there was a big chimney at each end of the house. The room had a second door which opened into a dirt-floored root cellar. On the floor above there were two rooms—a bedroom with an ancient iron ring for a knocker, and another dim room that had heavy oak doors at each side. One door opened to the ground level of the hillside. And the other was nailed shut above an eight-foot drop where once there had been an outside stairway. The marks still showed on the wall. Above that, under a gambrel roof, was an attic littered with broken lamp chimneys, old rags, and pieces of a bicycle. Here the beams were somewhat smaller and were held in place by wooden pegs. There was no electricity, no telephone, and very little plumbing.

But—the walls were two feet thick, the windows were deeply recessed and had small panes of wavy handblown glass. There were massive oak beams, floor boards that were at least ten inches wide, paneled oak shutters, and in the living room a fieldstone fireplace big enough to stand up in. The cupboards and the inside doors had "H" and "L" hinges we subsequently learned stood for Holy Lord and were good for keeping witches and evil spirits away.

It was not exactly love at first sight. It took me two trips from top to bottom and about twenty-five minutes. Here was a Cinderella of a house waiting to be cherished and loved and put to rights.

With the house went sixty acres of land and the owner wouldn't sell the house without it. We didn't want the land, but we did want the house. The price was six thousand dollars for all of it. With a mortgage Howard could just afford it. He made a down payment and gave me the place for a present. By the time we left I knew I would unwall the kitchen fireplace, put red calico curtains on the windows, and make the attic into two bedrooms.

Howard was working very hard at this time and I had been ill so it was May before we saw our house again. When we rounded the bend in the long lane our astonished eyes beheld a world exploded into blossom. The place floated in apple blossoms. On that stark, wintry day when we had acquired it we didn't even realize we had bought trees—and here was our little house set down in the middle of an orchard. A fountain of pink and white almost masked the front of the house. I put my arms around its huge trunk and sniffed the air and looked up into its branches. I had never thought of a tree as being something that could be owned personally. But this was my tree—mine—mine. I owned it. The deed said so. It was my tree.

Of course there were other trees that we discovered as the year went on. There was the one with branches that touched the ground all around. We called it "the tent" and we could sit under it in the rain and not get wet, the one we hung the swing from, and the Chinese mulberries that were strangers to this part of the country and must have been brought there long ago by some voyager returning from the Orient. There were maples that turned crimson and tulip trees that turned gold, and all the dogwoods, and all the trees that were good for climbing, hundreds of them, but that first apple tree, the present from Howard, was always my special tree.

We found we had also bought a brook. It ran quite close to

the house, slipped under a small bridge and then spread out into a duck pond that reflected the willow tree and the moon and the stars.

Of course New York remained our home, but now we also had a lovely little holiday house and a piece of country as well.

Russel Crouse came into our lives. It would seem appropriate that someone who was to be so important to us should have made a star entrance with flags flying and trumpets blowing. But that was not the way it happened.

At that time Russel was press agent for the Theatre Guild. He had been a newspaperman, had had his own column on the *Post*. He was a nostalgia buff and the author of three very good books—*It Seems Like Yesterday*, *Mr. Currier and Mr. Ives*, and *American Keepsake*, all beautifully written and beautifully illustrated with pictures of the period. He had also written *Murder Won't Out* about unsolved murder cases. He was married to Alison Smith, a newspaperwoman and a very pretty and bright one. She was assistant drama critic on the *Globe* and later on the *World*. Russel never drank anything alcoholic, but Alison drank enough to make up for it. He never tried to change her; in fact, when they were at home he was the one to mix the cocktails. Buck (everyone called him Buck) was a darling man—generous and funny and kind. He loved puns, the worse the better. He always looked somewhat rumpled. I felt as if I had known him forever.

Actually he entered our lives by way of a dream. Cole Porter had been spending the weekend with Neysa McMein at her Long Island home. She was the fine painter who did so many wonderful illustrations and magazine covers, and Buck was one of her many friends. Cole described the situation to her, which was as follows: Vinton Freedley was producing a musical by P. G. Wodehouse and Guy Bolton, and muisc by Cole Porter. (The original book was written by Bolton and Wodehouse; all the songs were by Cole Porter.) On the strength of these three important names he had been able to sign up Ethel Merman, Victor Moore, William Gaxton, and

Bettina Hall—and Howard Lindsay as director. Several of the songs had already been written, but the book was not yet finished. When it finally arrived, Freedley was bitterly disappointed and realized that it would all have to be done over again. He begged Howard to rewrite it, but Howard said he couldn't possibly take on that extra job without the help of a collaborator. Neysa McMein had had a dream that Buck was the perfect collaborator. She had told this to Cole the next day.

The original show took place on an ocean liner and the climax of the comedy was to be a shipwreck. It was called *Bon Voyage*. At about this time the *Morro Castle*, returning from a cruise, caught fire at sea and over one hundred lives were lost. Obviously this was not the time for the forthcoming comedy.

Because of Freedley's previous commitment to Wodehouse and Bolton, it meant that the playwrights Lindsay and Crouse would get only one half of 1 per cent of royalties, but at least Howard had his salary as director and Buck still had his press-agent job with the Guild. They worked like fiends day and night, but by the time they left with the company for the Boston tryout, the last act had not been finished. No one in the company knew it. They worked all the way on the train up to Boston, and after we had checked in at the hotel they continued to work. I saw little of my husband those days except when he staggered to bed. One night they wrote, literally, all night long, and I didn't see Howard until he came down to have breakfast with me the next morning. After breakfast he went directly to rehearsal.

The new musical *Anything Goes* opened complete with a last act. It was an instant success. Boston loved it, and New York loved it even more. It was the musical hit of 1934 and ran for 420 performances on Broadway.

In 1935, Howard produced a comedy that he had written with Damon Runyon. It was a dramatization of one of Runyon's stories and was called *A Slight Case of Murder*. It concerned a wealthy ex-racketeer boss who has become a legitimate beer brewer. Every August he rents a big house during the Saratoga racing season. He discovers that the top-floor room holds the bodies of four hijackers who had belonged to an enemy mob of his racketeering days. The question is how to get rid of the bodies without getting himself mixed up with the law. It was a hilariously funny and rowdy show, but it did not get the good reviews from the critics that it well deserved. It closed after only sixty-nine performances. This was the last play that Howard ever wrote without Russel Crouse as collaborator.

While I was sorting out the contents of the living-room chest of drawers, all the things my burglars had left scattered on the floor, I came across an envelope containing verses that I had written when I was very young. Some of them had been published in magazines, and some of them that go back as far as 1926 were used in Walter Winchell's columns. Here are the verses that describe in astonishing detail the house that did not come into being until so many years later.

SOMEDAY

I want the quaintest little house
Beyond the quaintest little town,
Beside a little lake so clear
You see the trees all upside down.
I want it weather-beaten gray,
The color of a rainy day.

'Twill have a meadow for a lawn,
Where meadow grass with clover mingles,
And it will have a rambler rose
To blossom on its nice gray shingles,
And in its doorway there will be
A lovely russet apple tree.

'Twill have a pleasant living room
With cozy little window nooks;
A colored room for dismal days,
A room to hold my favorite books;
A fireplace for a snowy night,
Luster tea set—candle light.

A bedroom just beneath the roof,
Where in the night I'll hear the rain,
And feel so snug, so safe and warm
The while it splashes on the pane.
Beneath the quilt I'll cuddle deep,
And let it sing me sound asleep.

My house will have a kitchen, too;
A kitchen clean and blue and white,
A path of stones with grass between,
A doorstep where I'll sit at night
To watch the moon come up and make
A bridge of gold across the lake.

I want someone to share my house
And make it quite complete, you see;
Someone who's fond of foolishing,
Who'll live and love and laugh with me:
And when there's firelight on the wall
I think we will not talk at all.

After we got the farm I started keeping a diary. Why does one keep a diary, I wonder? It must be because sometimes life gives one moments so beautiful that somehow an effort must be made to hold on to them—to save them from oblivion by writing them down—and moments so terrifying and secret that they could not be confided to anyone, and yet must, simply must, be somehow expressed. With me the secret and terrifying moments came later in my life. They were written down and then hidden or destroyed. I remember burning pages in the fireplace.

Here is the first entry in my diary on June 15, 1935: "I bought this diary to start the good life—to check up on myself—I may make progress as a person (I hope)—I really must get out of this rut of physical illness and mental lethargy somehow. I am taking insulin (to make me eat) and seeing two doctors and a dentist at present. I *must* stop thinking and talking about how awful I feel. It may help me and it will certainly help the man I live with—poor Howard. I didn't get to sleep until after four last night. The damned intestinal constriction. Oops! Here I go again!"

June 17th: "I made iced tea and sandwiches for Howard and Buck this afternoon. Howard and I drove out to the farm last night. The little house looked beautiful. We could see its lights across the fields half a mile before we got there. Inside looks terrible."

July 9, 1935: "I am here alone. Beautiful rain tonight. I watched and listened from the living room and then went upstairs to the bedroom that used to be an attic and lay on the bed to enjoy hearing the rain on the roof.

> "A bedroom just beneath the roof
> Where in the night I'll hear the rain."

"Funny the way dreams come true. My house has given me the most real happiness I have had all year. I love it so, and it is beginning to look right, and I have great plans for it for next spring. Owning a house and a garden must be very much like having a child and watching it grow and develop. Howard and I went for a drive last night in the Ford and got lost, which is what we like to do. Got home very late and ended at the garage door with a loud rendition of 'Night and Day.'"

October 2, 1935: "I painted the kitchen today. Hope to finish it tomorrow. I am here in the living room by myself, with the clock ticking and the fire crackling, and the cat purring. What a summer this has been! Happy for the most part in such a different way than I have ever been happy before. No excitement of the kind I'd have thought I couldn't get along without—but watching, really for the first time—Nature, Weather, Growing Things. No personal ambition, no personal vanity, no plans for the future except for the future of my house and garden, literally living only one day at a time. For the first time in my life I haven't wanted to act; in fact, I have wanted not to act, also for the first time in my life. I guess I'm afraid to. Only once in a while when I read a good play or see a good performance the desire comes back a little. I wonder if it has gone for good? I am better physically now at the end of the summer. Have had lots of times of feeling ill, but out here it hasn't seemed important. It hasn't stopped my doing things that I wanted to do (unlike all those other times when I have gotten sick during the run of a play). Probably, because for the first time ever my wants have been very simple. They haven't been the driving kind. To dig in the garden, to sit under the trees, to explore the fields, to decorate the house. Howard comes out as often as he can and of course these are the best times of all."

October 4, 1935: "Howard phoned me at the farm today that he has paid off the last mortgage on the farmhouse. I own it outright now and it is a wonderful feeling. It is really mine and nothing can take it away from me. Everything is clear and settled and paid for. God bless Howard. God bless God. Hurray!"

October 20, 1935: "The beautiful feeling of well-being has worn off. But even having had it for one day—yesterday—was worth a lot. Still, yesterday reminded me of the way it felt to be well, and I am more than ever impatient with this chronic state of negative health. What the hell is the matter with me? I wish I knew. Or I wish the doctors knew. Or I wish *somebody* knew. When I have responsibilities to meet in the theatre I seem to crumple up. One doctor told me that I was not physically equipped for the theatre. Why didn't I try living within my limitations? Why didn't I move to the country and raise dogs?"

November 9, 1935: "Howard came out last night. He told me about the story he and Damon Runyon are going to make into a play. *A Slight Case of Murder.* It sounds wonderful. We read Gerald du Maurier all evening. The chrysanthemums are just about through blooming, but of all things, the petunias don't even know it is November. They are as gay as they were in June. Hunting season opened today, guns popping from daylight on. We will get back to town in a hurry."

November 12, 1935: "Went to see the doctor. He said he was glad I had claustrophobia. Said it was a good sign. What the hell does that mean? I feel vile, depressed, tired, and *vile.* Sometimes I think there is only one class of people in the world stupider than Christian Scientists and that is doctors. I don't know why I keep going to them—now it begins all over again—doctor, dentist, doctor. Oh, hell! How I dread it, and yet I keep on going to them in the desperate faith, or maybe I should say hope, that sometime they will do something for me —damn! The worst of it is that I feel so ashamed of myself for being sick so much. I wonder how I'll feel a year from today? Hope I'll be alive because I'd hate to miss seeing things bloom on the farm."

November 29, 1935: "We took a walk across the fields today. It seemed so good when Howard and I were finally alone. We both want our friends to see and love the farm as we do, and we often have guests. We have had so few times by ourselves. How I wish he could get a couple of weeks off—just to stay here, with no company, but Howard is so busy still with *A Slight Case of Murder.* It opened but didn't come off as well with the critics as it deserved to. It is a wonderfully good show, terribly funny.

"In the evening we read Joseph Verner Reed's book *The Curtain Falls,* an altogether grand book. Seems odd that a book about complete disillusionment should make me eager and excited about the theatre again. I don't dare be excited. I will just be a happy vegetable. Howard was very sweet. He assured me that I wouldn't ever be a vegetable, or if I was it would be a vegetable as sweet and fragrant as a flower. The darling. We talked about acting together someday and about his writing the Washington play, and it was all very nice and dim and cozy and sheltered."

(The Washington play turned to be *State of the Union* ten years later, by Lindsay and Crouse. It won them the Pulitzer Prize.)

I have entirely forgotten to mention that I did pictures in Hollywood once in a while, during those years when I was in and out of the theatre so much. The parts were small and usually unimportant. After I first arrived on the New York scene, I was offered contracts by the major studios, but they were all term contracts of five or seven years, and I had not the slightest interest in being a picture actress. It was the habit of the studios to sign up any young persons who had distinguished themselves on Broadway, but I wanted only the theatre and was not willing to stay on the Coast more than a few weeks at a time. One of my first parts, and probably the only really good part I ever played there, was in a musical extravaganza called *Murder at the Vanities*. It was also the first part in Hollywood pictures for Carl Brisson (the Continental matinee idol), and for the beautiful and talented Kitty Carlisle who was later to marry Moss Hart.

Howard too went to the Coast from time to time to do a writing job. Sometimes we were there simultaneously. He had no more real interest in pictures than I did.

Twice while we were together at the Chateau Elysee we experienced a small earthquake which, out there, is politely called "a trembler." The first time was when we had been out very late at a party the night before. At about eight o'clock in the morning I was awakened by the tinkling of the glass prisms on the wall brackets and the shaking of the room. I reached over to the next bed, nudged Howard, and said, "Dearie, we are having an earthquake." He simply opened one baleful eye and said quite sternly, "Dorothy, I have just got to get some sleep." Our second small earthquake was in another year and it happened in the middle of the afternoon. The Chateau Elysee was one of the few high buildings in Hollywood. A number of us were standing by the elevator waiting to be taken to safety when down the hall came a British actor who had been there for a few months. His bathrobe was flying out behind him and he was saying in a loud voice, "This is the last straw!"

I went to Hollywood again in January 1936. I had my same lovely room at the Chateau Elysee. We had an impromptu New Year's Eve party—Jimmy Stewart, Kent Smith, my treasured old friend Gladys Hurlbut, and Rachel Crothers, the popular playwright. We took our champagne to the roof to toast the New Year. Jimmy had his banjo and played "Ragtime Cowboy Joe." The name of the picture I acted in was *And So They Were Married*. The stars were Mary Astor and Melvyn Douglas. My dear friend Elliott Nugent was the director. The picture was about two people who got snowbound in a small country inn, and thereby hangs the romance.

My diary of February 1936 records that we went to Lake

Tahoe to shoot the snow scenes. Tahoe is very high in the mountains, and we got caught in a terrible blizzard. It started the day we were shooting in the Cal-Neva Lodge, a summer resort hotel which is even higher up the mountain than Tahoe. They phoned from headquarters to get us out and back down to Tahoe quickly. It was a terrifying drive down a steep mountainside through blinding snow. I discovered the door to my cottage had blown open and my bed and chest of drawers and trunk were covered with snow. Some of the men helped dig me out, and I got a fire started in my little wood stove, and we all had a drink of gin.

February 10, 1936: "Still blizzarding. Mary Astor, Elliott Nugent, and the head cameraman all down with the flu. One hundred people here on location and no doctor. Telephone wires are down and we are completely snowbound, no one can get in or out. Food is getting low, but fortunately there is plenty of liquor."

February 20, 1936: "We are now back in Hollywood. The blizzard finally stopped. We had been completely snowbound for ten days. A doctor was flown in from Truckee, ten miles down the mountain. The sick people were taken out in ambulances, and the rest of us were finally dug out, and telephone wires restored. I stood in line to get word to Howard—had visions of his being frantic with worry about me. He told me he hadn't been worried at all because he thought it was a publicity stunt. They are ending by shooting all the snow scenes here in the studio—with cornflakes. We had to do the scenes shot at Cal-Neva Lodge all over again because it had been so cold there that our breath showed.

Between *Another Language*, which was 1932, until February 1937, the only stage appearances I made were in two Players Club revivals which each played for only one week. They were *Milestones* and *The County Chairman*. I turned down several plays because I was so afraid I would get sick again and spoil things. I had a terrible sense of guilt, and I had had to leave plays so many times that I was getting the reputation of being unreliable. I didn't dare accept a part because I was afraid of failing, not only the play but myself.

My diary entry of June 21, 1936, reads: "I had a lovely birthday on the farm, complete with roses and fireflies. Howard gave me coral earrings. But as far as Howard is concerned it has been my birthday all year. Instead of a cake, we had a birthday pie made out of our first cherries."

June 22, 1936: "Howard stayed last night. Perfect midsummer day today. July lilies just beginning, delphiniums in their prime. But things never grow fast enough to suit me. I worked like mad today and tonight Howard and I just wandered around outside, looking at everything. I saw the first evening star and was so happy I couldn't think of anything to wish for. I hope there are several more lives to be lived after this one, because I can't possibly crowd enough living into one lifetime."

October 12, 1936: "Came up from Boston to town tonight. Howard feeling fine when I left. *Red, Hot and Blue* looks very good. They have Ethel Merman, Jimmy Durante, and Bob Hope. I had never seen Bob Hope before. He is good. One of the chorus girls asked me if I used to be on the stage. I said, yes, and went to bed feeling depressed."

October 30, 1936: "*Red, Hot and Blue* opened here last night. Notices more good than bad. The book was panned a bit and some of the critics said the music was not up to Cole Porter's standard. (Cole tells me they have said that about everything he ever wrote except two shows, and one of them was *Anything Goes.*) Gabriel gives it a rave and Winchell calls it a bore. 'Delicious, Delightful, De-Lovely' is a de-lovely song and so are the others."

Diary entry of November 2, 1936, reads: "We drove around back-country roads last night through the softest, warmest, dreamiest night imaginable. The sort of night that makes you want to sing songs softly and to drive slowly. We have been completely unambitious, doing nothing but reading and driving."

November 3, 1936: "Drove to High Bridge this morning to vote for Roosevelt. Beautiful autumn weather. Tonight we listened to the radio and were delighted with the landslide, of course. Biggest presidential majority in 116 years—46 out of 48 states. Howard read me *Green Mansions*."

Howard and I had often dreamed that someday we could have a New York house of our own. The house directly back of our little duplex apartment had a lovely garden. It boasted a big poplar tree and a little fountain which spouted water from a cast-iron lily. We used to admire it from our terrace. One night when we were taking a walk we found ourselves in front of the brownstone that the garden belonged to. I said, "Howard, why don't we ask if by any chance this house is for sale?" Howard said, "Good Lord, Dorothy, you just can't walk up to someone's front door and ask if their house is for sale!" I said, "Why not? The worst thing that could happen is that the door might be shut in our faces." I took the lead and Howard followed reluctantly.

An Oriental butler answered our ring. I said, "We are Mr. and Mrs. Lindsay. Could we possibly speak to the owner of the house?" The butler beamed and said, "Please come in. I will tell Miss Hoyt that you are here." This wasn't quite what we had expected, but we sat down sheepishly in the parlor, feeling very apologetic. A beautiful white-haired lady, Miss Hoyt, came downstairs. We explained that we lived at 40 West Tenth Street and had so much admired her garden. We said our name was Lindsay and apologized for our intrusion, but we wanted to know if by any chance her house was for sale. She couldn't have been more charming. She said, "What an odd coincidence—I put it on the market only this morning." She said she would like to think of someone named Lindsay living in her house because her sister was Lady Lindsay, who lived in London. Of course that explained the butler being so cordial. He recognized the name as having some connection with Miss Hoyt. We bought the house and moved in the next spring.

———————

August 5, 1937: "Opened in Falmouth for the tryout of Gladys Hurlbut's *Lovers' Meeting*—same old terror, same old sickness. Must have given a rotten performance. Hope I didn't spoil it for Gladys. She's my oldest friend and I love her dearly. Howard and Buck and Alison have gone to Ireland and England for a holiday."

August 10, 1937: "Opened in Matunuck tonight. Bird got into the theatre and batted around the stage. Birds should stay in cages or in trees where they belong."

August 13, 1937: "This is our wedding anniversary. I am in Matunuck with *Lovers' Meeting*. Awfully sick and more nervous than I have been in years. Had hysterics all by myself this afternoon. The spasm in my stomach so bad that I thought I was dying of peritonitis, though I am not even sure what it is. I was feeling very tragic at the thought of dying in Matunuck while Howard is in Europe. And just at my lowest ebb there came a cable from him saying, 'London isn't any fun without you.' I decided to live after all."

The answer to my prayers appeared in 1938. Josh Logan and Paul Osborn were doing Paul's beautiful play called *On Borrowed Time*. I had been frightened about the theatre for such a long time, and now after all the parts I had had to turn down I was offered a part that surely I could play. It was the part of Granny, who dies in the first act and who has only one line at the very end of the play. Burns Mantle described the play as "A curiously happy and satisfying comedy about death. It is the fascinating story of an old man who chases Death up a tree and holds him there by magic, while he tries to find a proper home for his seven-year-old grandson who is an orphan." It is a love story between Gramps and Little Pud. Richard Bennett was Gramps, I was Granny, and Jean Adair was the mean aunt who wanted to adopt Pud because he had inherited money. Frank Conroy played Death in the person of Mr. Brink, a mild-mannered man in a business suit. Nothing can die until Gramps releases Mr. Brink from the apple tree, where he is held captive, until Gramps permits him to come down. Gramps has erected a high fence around the tree to keep people away from Death. Pud falls while trying to climb the fence; his back is broken and he will never walk again. Gramps releases Mr. Brink and begs him to come down and take them both. They go happily off to Eternity just as

Granny's voice is heard calling to them from the other side of death.

This was a short and undemanding part. If I was fit ever to do anything again in the theatre I was fit to do this. It didn't even matter if I got thin and haggard-looking because I was playing a very old lady. This was my chance to prove to myself that I could still be an actress. We rehearsed much longer than usual because Richard Bennett couldn't seem to learn his part. Whenever he went up in his lines he would stop rehearsal and make a speech about "the goddamn playwrights didn't know how to write the goddamn lines."

We went to New Haven for the tryout. Opening night there was pure actors' nightmare except that we were unfortunate enough to be awake. Richard Bennett didn't know a line of his part. Everyone, including Little Pud, gave him his lines. The curtain should have been rung down after the first act, but somehow we floundered through to the end and we closed that night. After a week or so we went into rehearsal with Dudley Digges as Gramps.

Howard was in California all this time doing a writing job and I didn't expect him back until spring when he had finished his work out there. I gave an opening-night party at our house. We telephoned Howard in Hollywood and all of us talked to him. We waited for the first reviews and they were simply great. Among my opening-night wires was one from Howard which I shall always treasure. It is put safely away in the metal strongbox which my burglars broke open in their search for valuables. This was a valuable that they didn't want. The wire was to Granny Stickney and it said simply, "Darling, I can hardly wait."

For a long time I had been searching and praying for understanding, and now I tried more desperately than ever to find some inner strength that would save me. I reread *Lessons in Truth*. I got out my Emerson and read "Self-Reliance," "Compensation," "The Over Soul," and "Spiritual Laws." I read my Bible. I stayed in the play for three months, getting weaker and weaker, going to the theatre every night with a book of

Emerson to bolster my courage, and a hot-water bottle concealed in a black bag, which I clung to every moment offstage to warm my icy hands. When the first act was over I would lie on a cot in my dressing room, hoping for strength enough to get up and say that last line when the time came.

In February the amazing thing happened. I am going to try to record it. It has grown dim now, but it will never be lost to me as long as I can hold close even the memory of its brilliance. I know of no words in the human language that are adequate to describe it, but I'll try.

On that morning I had reached the very bottom of despair. I realized that there was no outside help for me anywhere, and that if I survived, the help would have to come from within. But after the repeated failures I was empty of hope. Empty of everything. I simply stopped struggling and let go. I got out of bed and stood looking out the window at the poplar tree. Then—the incredible thing started happening. The thing that set that period of my life apart from all the rest of it.

It was like a door gradually opening—like a light, dim at first and then growing brighter and brighter until my whole being was illuminated. The door opened full and I saw the complete view. It was no longer believing in God. It was KNOWING. I knew with absolute certainty. It was a shining realization that I was of the same essence—an actual expression of all the good, the strength, the power, the love that is God. It was absolute assurance of infinity, or perhaps I should say eternity. Not eternity to come but eternity NOW, and I was at the center of it. I was no longer afraid. I was secure and safe. The fact that I was sick simply didn't matter. The bad things had no importance, no reality. All was good. There was no such thing as sin. Mistakes—and mistakes didn't matter either—but never sin. Perhaps mistakes had a place in the scheme of things and were necessary for the working out of a plan. I was one with the universe and everything in it—with people and animals and trees and inanimate objects, and I loved it all passionately. The whole world was indescribably beautiful. All pressures were gone. I felt unhurried, perhaps for the first time in my life, and yet there was tremendous excitement and glory. It was as though I possessed a new sense—beyond any of the human senses I had known before. It was an illumination that one could no more encompass in words than one could describe color to the blind or sound to the deaf. It was like being in love—only more wonderful. It gave a color, a shine to everything, as love does. This radiance and rapture lasted over a few weeks—three or four perhaps, not continuously (I doubt that one could have lived continuously at that pitch of ecstasy) but intermittently, and after that at longer intervals. I would wake in the mornings—not slowly but suddenly—bright awake with such joy growing and expanding inside me that I could hardly contain it. A smile would start deep down before it came to the surface of my face. I sang as I dressed. When the radiance was the brightest inside it must have shown through because sometimes I would notice in the mirror that I actually *looked* different. Smooth skin and bright eyes and all look of strain gone.

One morning I looked out the window and saw that lovely tree was coming into leaf seemingly overnight. I realized that that was what was happening to me, that I was part of the same plan. I began to feel a little better, even physically. It was less hard to eat, and I didn't go to the theatre with such dread. Several times I gave my performance easily and with none of the numb, sick terror I had had.

One night, riding alone to the theatre in a taxi, I had a vivid realization of the kinship of all human beings—the taxi driver, the other actors, the people walking on the streets—that I was one with them and that we were all part of the same great idea and that I *loved* them all. We passed an old drunken derelict and I longed to stop the cab and tell him that I loved him.

I was still sick, but the strange thing was that it didn't matter. There was the assured feeling that I would be well sometime, but above and beyond that it didn't even matter if I wasn't, or even if other misfortunes came. Nothing could destroy me *inside* if I could only keep my gates open to this wonderful awareness, and keep in touch as long as I could with this new source of supply.

While Howard was in Hollywood I used to mind coming home to an empty house. But I enjoyed being alone these days. I loved coming home from the theatre and reading Emerson with a clear understanding of what he wrote, and a quick response to his words and thoughts. Sometimes the light was bright as sunlight and sometimes dim as a candle, but it was there. Occasionally there were discouraged days and frightened days even during these weeks.

For a long time Howard had been phoning me from California that he wanted me to go to see a certain doctor. The very thought of another doctor was almost more than I could bear, but this was a kind of doctor I had never seen before. He called himself a neurologist, not a psychiatrist. His name was Irving Pardee. I didn't think for a minute he could help me— but with this new inner knowledge and security I knew he couldn't *hurt* me. And Howard, phoning from the Coast, had said, "If you love me you'll do this for me." So of course I went. Then too, I thought that this might be part of the plan for me and that I should keep all doors open and that I would receive good from this source too.

The first time I went I liked his face but was much too nervous to have any clearer impression than that. He looked kind and tired. As I gradually got to know him I discovered a rare human being. He had an inner quiet and poise and humor and devotion to his work. And something that goes beyond understanding—an intuitive something.

Dr. Pardee asked me about my childhood. I told him that I had had a perfectly normal, happy childhood, and I really believed what I was saying. I had succeeded in blocking out so completely the things I did not want to remember—the dark rooms, the operations, the deaths of my mother and father— that I really believed I was telling him the truth. It took some time and many sessions before the doctor could unearth these experiences, these facts. This must have been a beginning of my cure, though the completion was still a long way off.

Howard was coming home soon now and I was spending all my spare time and energy getting ready for him. He must have been due about the first of May. I was surprising him by having his study fixed, having the old paint taken off the beautiful pine paneling, new slipcovers made for the furniture, fresh ivy for the gilt wall brackets; the new Capehart record player was a surprise too. At a downtown market I had bought lots of pink geraniums and blue ageratum for the garden border and four enormous blue hydrangeas for the four corners. Howard came back on a warm spring day, and then I collapsed completely. I lay in bed for several weeks, not moving or wanting to move. The most utter, complete exhaustion that had in it a sort of peace, a sigh of relief at having given up all effort. The weather was warm and lovely, my room was clean and pretty, my nightgowns were cool, and I could watch the beautiful tree without even moving my head.

During this time Howard and Buck were talking over *Life With Father* in the library down the hall. They were outlining the play and having a hilarious time of it. All this was being done strictly on speculation, as they had not yet gotten the rights from the widow of Clarence Day, Jr.

We decided to go on a North Cape cruise with Russel and Alison. We couldn't afford it but we went anyway. We all knew Hilmer Lundbeck, the son of the owner of the *Kungsholm*, the ship on which we were sailing. We all sat at one table and had a gay time. There was one small inconvenience —I was on crutches part of the time. I had finished my chores of packing and had put on a new dress and a new hat and had gone down to say hello and good-bye to the cast of *On Borrowed Time*. I was feeling very happy. I missed the last step of the stairs outside my old dressing room, fell and sprained my ankle. I sat on the floor and laughed. It was all so ridiculous. I wondered if this was a way of my being told I had better keep out of theatres. Dr. Pardee bandaged me the next morning and gave me a pair of crutches, and we sailed at five that afternoon. Howard and Russel did a lot of talking about *Life With Father* while we were away.

We spent a day each in Norway, Sweden, Denmark, Iceland, and Finland, and loved them all. Then we went to Russia, starry-eyed and open-armed, to see what this wonderful new Russia was like since the Revolution. When we reached

Leningrad, Russel got his landing permit without delay, but the visas were denied to Alison, Howard, and me. Apparently visas were given out on the eeny-meeny-miney-mo system. We were, to say the least, puzzled. But Hilmer Lundbeck was furious. He phoned someone in Moscow and we were given our landing visas immediately.

The Russians made it very plain that they didn't want us—in fact, ours was the last cruise ship allowed in before the Iron Curtain descended. We had three days there. Alison and I stayed in Leningrad and Howard and Buck went on to Moscow. The day after they arrived, there was a sports celebration and a parade in Red Square. They were given their choice of being locked in their hotel for the day or being taken far away to see a new dam. They chose the dam.

We all played a game of smiling at people to try to make them smile back, but they never did. We went to Tsarskoe Selo, which was the summer palace of the Czar and his family. It was being kept intact, exactly as they had lived in it, and it was being used as a propaganda museum. The palace was a frame building, a curious combination of very simple rooms that looked lived in, and very formal rooms with a lot of malachite and gold—obviously for state occasions. We first went through the living room that looked as if it had been furnished from Grand Rapids. In one corner was a green felt table with a stained-glass chandelier over it. On the table was a shoe box. When the guide's attention was elsewhere, I reached over and looked inside. It was someone's collection of picture postcards. On another table was the Czarina's half-finished sewing with a threaded needle stuck in a pincushion and open scissors beside it. Everywhere were framed snapshots of the family. The little girls in their white communion dresses, the Czarevitch in his enormous white shako, photographs signed "To Nicky, with love." In the Czarina's bedroom the wall was entirely covered with religious icons; of course, one immediately thought of Rasputin and the hold he had had over the superstitious Czarina. In the very formal library there was a double staircase leading to more books on a balcony above, and under the stairway I saw, of all things, a child's kiddy car.

In the entryway we saw the little gilt chairs that the family had sat on before being taken out and murdered. The propaganda had worked exactly the way the Russians had not intended—it backfired. One only felt terribly sorry for the royal family.

When we sailed out of port the ship suddenly listed far to one side. Everyone ran to the deck to see why. A Russian destroyer had suddenly cut across our bow in a gesture that said plainly: "We are powerful here, so don't fool with us—just get out!"

When the Clarence Day stories of *Life With Father* started coming out in *The New Yorker* magazine, Howard and I read them aloud to each other with pure delight. They were stories of the Days' family life in their Madison Avenue brownstone in the early eighties. It was a life dominated by Father (or so he thought) who talked back loudly to the newspapers when he didn't agree with them, and who could never understand why God made so many damn fools and Democrats. Clarence Day, Sr., was Clare, and his wife, Lavinia, was called Vinnie.

Howard thought the stories would be rich material for a play—a period comedy. Buck agreed. But when they started making inquiries they found that Oscar Serlin, who had yet to make his reputation as a Broadway producer, had had the same thought and had already talked to the widow of Clarence Day, Jr., about the rights, as she owned all the rights to *The New Yorker* stories. She consented to let him try to get a play made, but with no commitment on her part.

Oscar Serlin had gotten the screenwriter Allan Scott to do a script. He wrote a script, obviously intended for pictures, in which W. C. Fields was to play Father. Mrs. Day took one horrified look and turned it down flatly. Serlin met with Mrs. Day once more and she agreed to let him try to find another writer, and if he could come up with a suitable play she and the rest of the Day family would read it and then decide whether or not they would let it be done. This time, Serlin asked Howard Lindsay to write the play, and he accepted joyfully, with Russel Crouse as collaborator. They had written three musicals prior to this: *Anything Goes, Red, Hot and Blue,* and *Hooray for What!* They were afraid they were beginning to be thought of as only book writers for musicals. It was high time they wrote a straight play.

When we returned from the North Cape cruise we were very, very broke. Howard was offered a large sum of money to go to the Coast and do a picture. We talked it over and both decided that it would be much more important to stay in New York and write a play. So we mortgaged everything we could and borrowed money from the bank in Dickinson, North Dakota. From then on the play was our main concern. I was going to Dr. Pardee and that was expensive. Also, neither Howard nor Buck had any income, nor did they have any rights to the Clarence Day stories.

Their method of work never varied through the years. They would meet every afternoon in our library and would outline the whole play in detail, and decide exactly what was to go in every scene and what the overall structure of the play would be before they put a word of dialogue down on paper. After they had talked and planned all afternoon they would often call each other up at night. This became such a routine procedure that one night I heard Howard dial the Crouse number and say, "This is Buck, I want to speak to Howard." Conversations were started in the middle of a sentence ". . . and it would be much better if . . . etc., etc." They had mapped it out to the smallest detail. The actual dialogue took them less than three weeks.

The dreaded day came when they must meet the Day family and show them what they had worked on for nearly two years. The audience consisted of Mrs. Clarence Day, her brother-in-law, and his wife. He was George Parmley Day who was the treasurer of Yale University. So the boys journeyed to New Haven. Howard read the first act, which was all they had written down, and he filled in the outlines of the rest of the play. The Days listened and said nothing, and Lindsay and Crouse came back to New York very discouraged.

But in less than a week they had the acceptance and approval of the Days and the rights to *The New Yorker* stories.

We all thought we should have stars to play Father and Mother. Getting a star to play Vinnie was not such a problem as Oscar Serlin had always had me in mind for the part. The script was offered to Alfred Lunt and Lynn Fontanne who turned it down. It was offered to Walter Huston who also turned it down, as did Walter Connelly, Roland Young, and John Halliday. The play was sent to many prospective investors but very few wanted to put money in *Life With Father*. Finally it was decided the play would be tried out for one week in Lakewood near Skowhegan, Maine, with Howard and me trying ourselves out in the parts of Father and Mother.

During the time that they were working I took one trip to Hollywood to do a Hitchcock picture for television. The old terror came back, but I knew I had to go anyway. I had been seeing Dr. Pardee for months, and a most peculiar thing was happening to me. I had begun to cry and couldn't stop. I was not sad and I was not crying about anything. The tears seemed to take over automatically and with no reason and no warning. It was as though all the crying I had not done through my childhood and in the past had finally caught up with me. All the tears that had been denied for so long had now taken possession. I might be at a party having a very good time when suddenly Niagara would overtake me and I would have to run to the nearest bathroom and shut myself in until the tears stopped. I came home rather proud of myself for having survived the flood.

In the summer we went to Lakewood, Maine, a place so full of happy memories for us, to try out the play and to try out ourselves in the parts of Father and Mother. I dared not tell even Howard—oh, least of all Howard—of my secret fears and doubts of my own capabilities. How terrible it would be if I let Howard down. I didn't. We played for one week. A number of people came up from New York to see it. They seemed to like it, but there was no great enthusiasm. One self-appointed critic told us we might have a good play if we left out everything about Father's baptism.

Howard tried wearing a false mustache but it kept coming off so he gave that up and started growing his own. We both gave good performances, and there was surprisingly little work to be done on the play. The four red-headed sons were all brought up from New York with us. They were Clarence, Jr., John, Whitney, and little Harlan. Jackie Devereaux played Clarence, and a gangly youth named Dick Simon played John, the next in line. Dick Simon had not stopped growing and his voice was changing. In the scene where Father tells him he will not get one cent of allowance until he has bought back all the patent medicine he has sold, there is a pause while John counts up. Then he says, in horror, "I'll be twenty-one years old!" His voice cracked in the middle of the line and he ended with a squeak. The audience roared. We kept it in permanently. Our youngest boy, who had never been on the stage before, was delighted with the audience laughter—he turned around and joined right in with them. We had to tell him that actors weren't supposed to know when the audience thought they were funny.

When the week's tryout was over we drove home by way of Vermont and took the walk we had taken so many years ago, following the brook through the woods from Tyson to Nineveh.

Back in New York Howard and I rehearsed our lines wherever we happened to be. One day we were in Longchamps having a cocktail. We were rehearsing the "account scene" where Clare and Vinnie are hotly quarreling. Before long we became aware that people were staring at us and listening to our spirited argument, probably saying to each other, "Wouldn't you think people would do their fighting at home instead of in a public place?" We were a little more careful after that.

Stewart Chaney designed a beautiful set for us. It was a copy of the morning room in the original Day house which once stood on Madison Avenue. It was complete down to the last Victorian geegaw. He even had copies made of two Day family portraits to hang on the wall.

I thought it might be funny to have Mother dressed all in

white for Father's baptism. The dress was made of beautiful white open-work eyelet embroidery. In fact, two of them were made, and every second week one was sent to a special hand laundry to be taken apart, washed, ironed, and put together again. The costume was so fresh and so pretty it sometimes got a hand when I came down the stairs wearing it. I had seven beautiful costumes and two beautiful red wigs. Howard also wore a red wig, and the four boys had their hair dyed bright red.

We all thought that we had a nice, amusing, well-written little play that might run for six months or, with good luck, even for eight. We thought that when we had exhausted all the audiences who were admirers of the Clarence Day stories we would close.

We played for a week in Baltimore before coming into New York. One Baltimore critic described the story this way: "In his own house Father is dictator—he thinks—but Mother, in spite of her patience and willing devotion, knows how to get the last word when the last word is worth fighting for. In Father's stubborn refusal to be baptized (his parents had been freethinkers) she finds such a cause. When the awful fact of his never having been baptized comes out quite casually, Mother simply refuses to believe this incredible information. 'Oh, that's ridiculous, Clare! Everyone is baptized. Why no one would keep a little baby from being baptized!"

The review continued: "Father goes to church as a matter of course but refuses to kneel. He utters a rousing 'Damn!' or two when the minister comes to call, and on the Sunday morning when the minister rebukes him from the pulpit, the red-haired broker rises and stalks out—his views on religion are not strictly orthodox.

"The sudden realization that Father is nameless in the sight of the Church is too much for Vinnie. She is sure that Father cannot go to heaven unless he has been baptized. She says to visiting Cousin Cora, 'Why I couldn't go to Heaven without Clare! I get lonesome for him even when I go to Ohio! I am not sure that in the sight of the Church we are even really married!' Father, after heroic resistance, is driven away in an expensive handsome cab to be sprinkled and given a name. The play is a prolonged squabble of all sorts of household and spiritual matters, but this never disturbs the unwavering bond of affection between these two redheads, and this is one of the reasons the play is such a joy to watch. The Days are a warm, rich, quarrelsome and affectionate family."

We were working very hard. Playing comedy takes much more vitality than playing a straight part, and *Life With Father* demanded all the vitality we could muster. Howard with his explosive "Oh God!" when things did not go his way, me, with running up- and downstairs. Vinnie rushes to Father every time he explodes and asks breathlessly, "What's the matter, Clare? What's wrong?" I made twenty-four trips up and down those stairs at each performance; I had eight quick changes of costume, and got in and out of my wigs five times.

There was a blessing on that play from the start—we had a fine producer in the person of Oscar Serlin and a fine director in the person of Bretaigne Windust, a beautiful production, and our great good fortune to get the Empire Theatre in New York to play it in. It wasn't quite the period of *Life With Father* but almost. The Empire had been built for Charles Frohman in 1893 to his own specification and with great elegance. It had a large white marble outer lobby lined with photographs of the great who had played there through the years, and a lovely large inner lobby where people could stroll and chat between acts, and look at the paintings of actors and actresses gilt-framed against the crimson damask walls. The whole theatre was red and gold and crystal. There should be a law making it compulsory for all theatres to look exactly like that.

By the time we got to New York we were both tired to a frazzle. Opening night, instead of being the gay and glamorous occasion that opening nights are supposed to be, was more like a nightmare to Howard and me. We were sitting glumly in the living room in that awful vacuum that occurs while you wait to go to the theatre and face that opening-night audience. Just then, a fire engine went screaming by. Howard looked up and said regretfully, "It can't be the Empire. It's too far downtown." There were times when we almost wished it had been. It seemed to us that every possible disaster occurred that night. At the very beginning the maid dropped a loaded breakfast tray in the middle of the stage. I spent the first scene holding up my train, picking up pieces of broken dishes and bits of soggy toast and saying my lines. In the second scene the minister forgot a long and important speech. Poor Howard ad-libbed as best he could. In the last scene one of the little boys forgot his straw hat and went upstairs to his dressing room to get it, thereby missing the scene entirely. Poor Howard ad-libbed some more. Finally the curtain came down, but we were too tired even to go to Mrs. Clarence Day's opening-night party for the cast. We just staggered home and cried into our cornflakes and went to bed. The next day we discovered to our amazement that the play was a smash hit.

The next weeks were hectic. At that time came the frantic activity that always accompanies the first weeks of a big success—publicity, photographs, interviews, etc. One day shortly after we had opened, the publicity man for our show was sent to interview me in order to get my biography. It was then up to him to decide what parts of the story he wanted—to place a paragraph in a newspaper or an item in someone's column, or perhaps to use the whole story as a piece for a magazine. I had told Dr. Pardee I was dreading this interview. He said, "On your doctor's orders you are to tell him the complete story, not leaving out anything about your childhood or growing-up years." The man came. I told him my story in accordance with the doctor's orders. When he had gone I slammed the door and ran into the nearest bathroom and threw up. But it was over with. I had done it.

There were about three weeks of very hard work both in and out of the theatre, and then—the dreadful thing happened again. I woke up one morning too sick to go on that night. I had slipped back into the old pattern—the same old nausea, the same weakness, the same terror and despair. Dr. Pardee came down to see me. I said to him, hoping for some comfort, "Just because I have failed this time doesn't mean that I will fail in the next part." He answered me, "Yes, it does." My understudy went on that night. When Howard came back he went straight upstairs to his bedroom without stopping to say good night to me. I knew he must have been just as disgusted with me as I was with myself. All day I had thought about what the doctor said. I got out of bed at midnight and went down to the kitchen. I found some jello in a dish. I forced myself to eat it and keep it down. The next night I went back in the play. I was very shaky and ill, and I must have given a bad performance, but I was there.

I didn't get well all at once. It took a long time, but this was a beginning. I used to stand in the wings waiting for my entrance cue and hoping I would die before I had to take those two steps that would bring me in front of the audience. I ate what I could—soft things that were easy to swallow—soups, jello, mashed potatoes, things like that. I think what really saved me was that I was acting with Howard. He didn't understand my sort of illness, but he was patient and kind. He used to read to me before we went to bed. I prayed a lot, and I was beginning very slowly to find a way of coping with my fears. Through those days I didn't dare even take a nap for fear I would slide back and lose what control I was beginning to have. A turning point came in December, about Christmastime. I stopped being so frightened and was starting to actually like playing Vinnie and to feel at home in front of an audience.

I had learned one important thing—a thing that was to stand me in good stead for the rest of my life. When panic overtook me and I felt absolutely unable to go on I would tell myself, "You don't have to do the whole play—you don't even have to play the next scene—all you have to do is say the next line." Sometimes, during my life that was to come, all I could manage was to say the next line, but that sufficed.

I got well. Eating was no longer a problem. I gained back all the weight I had lost. As time went on I loved playing Vinnie and I loved playing opposite Howard. I got a lift of heart every time I opened the stage door and went into my beautiful dressing room. Dressing rooms are notoriously shabby—two straight chairs, a narrow makeup shelf, a mirror, lights, and hooks to hang clothes on. This was the room that Charles Frohman had designed for Maude Adams so long ago. It had a large dressing table with triple mirrors and a shelf that pulled out to make a writing desk; a white painted chest of drawers with a cupboard for wigs and hats; a closet with a white-leather door that opened with a brass chain and ring; a gilt-framed mirror from floor to ceiling; a sofa and two white painted chairs. I fixed it up the way I imagined it had been in Maude Adams' day—red carpet, a sofa covered with red velvet, and red velvet cushions for the two chairs. I think she would have approved.

I must have been playing Vinnie well because in the spring I was given the Barter Theatre Award for the season's best performance. The award was the idea of Robert Porterfield who ran the Barter Theatre in Abingdon, Virginia. I was in heady company, as the previous award had been given to Laurette Taylor, and the following year it was given to Ethel Barrymore. The award consisted of an acre of land on the side of a mountain near Abingdon, a Virginia ham, and a handsomely inscribed platter "To eat it off of." Mrs. Roosevelt made the presentation at a big luncheon in Town Hall. While we were waiting in the anteroom until it was time to go in and sit at the table on the dais, Mrs. Roosevelt kept trying to get behind me and I kept trying to get behind her. Finally she said, "No. You go ahead. It's your party and you should lead." So I did.

With the award came the responsibility of auditioning aspiring boys and girls to be given summer jobs at the Barter. Twenty young people had appointments for the audition; more than fifty showed up. I picked out the boy and the girl who I thought had the most talent. The girl must have left the theatre after her season at the Barter for I have never heard of her since. The boy remained an actor, and a fine one. His name is Gregory Peck.

Who would have dreamed that we would still be playing at the beautiful old Empire for five gloriously happy, hardworking years? The play was to go on for nearly three years after we left, thereby breaking all records for the length of run of any Broadway play. (Years later the musical *Fiddler on the*

Roof broke our record by one week.) People probably thought that Howard and I must be rolling in money, but by the end of our first year we had just managed to pay off our mortgages and return the money we had borrowed from the Dickinson bank to use while the play was being written.

Life With Father had a charming little three-piece orchestra —piano, violin, and drums—that played songs of the period for the overture and between the acts. At the end of the second act I had been singing acappella "Sweet Marie" which ends, "Every daisy in the dell knows my secret, knows it well, and yet I dare not tell Sweet Marie." The orchestra picked it up on my note as the curtain descended.

Every year on the anniversary of our opening a huge party was given. It filled both outer and inner lobbies and sometimes overflowed onto the stage. There were actors doing parodies of *Life With Father*—Danny Kaye was one of the entertainers that first year (and that was before anyone even knew that he was Danny Kaye). The parties glittered with celebrities. One of the photographs that I rescued from the floor after the burglary shows Gypsy Rose Lee, Oscar Levant, Mary Martin, Helen Hayes, and John Van Druten. What surprised us was that one of our own little boys from the play was around getting autographs. Helen Hayes said to him, "Bobby, why do you want those autographs? What do you do with them?" Bobby said, "I take them home and copy them in a book."

During the five years we were at the Empire we had twenty-eight children—and not a brat among them. The two youngest who played Harlan and Whitney had to be replaced quite often as they outgrew their clothes at an alarming rate.

Little Bobby got a bit bored and twice he called me Miss Stickney during a performance instead of Mother, so a rehearsal was called. Ruth Hammond who played Cousin Cora and I were standing in the wings waiting for our cue. Bobby was sitting at his backstage desk looking at a comic book. Ruth motioned to him and whispered, "Bobby, come on, it's nearly your entrance. Don't you know we're having this rehearsal for you?" Bobby replied, "Why, they don't have to have a rehearsal for me. Don't they know I'm the one who doesn't like rehearsals?"

In our first season we were chosen to give the command performance for President Roosevelt's birthday celebration. So on Sunday, January 28, 1940, we journeyed to Washington to play a performance that night. We were pretty tired, having done our week's work that ended with two shows on Saturday. We looked forward to a reviving drink to pick us up after we got there. On arriving at the hotel we learned with dismay that no liquor was served in Washington on Sunday. I wasn't much of a drinker but one good strong martini would calm my nerves and give me much needed energy. When performance time came I was as nervous as I had been at the opening in New York. Buck Crouse swears that when I left the stage after the second act he heard me mutter, "I wouldn't go through this again for the President of the United States!"

We were invited to supper at the White House. President Roosevelt had been wheeled in and was seated in his place before we were ushered to the dining room. We sat at small tables for four—Howard and Alison and I were seated with the President. I had gotten over all my nervousness by that time and was feeling relaxed and happy, but Alison was having the jitters. At one point she asked the President, "Who was the artichoke who designed the White House?" Then one of her hairpins fell in the soup. But in spite of everything we had a wonderful time. Mr. Roosevelt was a charming host. He talked about all sorts of things including a dam that had just been built in North Dakota, when he learned that that was my home state. Mrs. Roosevelt went from table to table visiting everyone. Altogether, it turned out to be a graceful occasion.

One day I was reading a script called *Bodies in Our Cellar*. It had been sent to me by Joseph Kesselring, its author, who wanted me for one of the parts in case I was ever willing to leave *Life With Father*. Howard watched with fascination as I read and laughed and gasped over it. I said, "Howard, this is the most outrageous and funniest play I ever read. There is an awful lot wrong with it, but the main characters and the idea are completely hilarious." Howard said, "I want to read it." He did and had the same reaction. It was a story of two darling old ladies who had only one slight idiosyncrasy—they disposed of lonely old gentlemen with their homemade elderberry wine laced with arsenic and buried them in their cellar. Howard called Buck and told him about it. He said, "This could be either a hit or a huge flop. But I think we ought to get it and produce it and do the rewriting ourselves. We can take out the unpleasant parts and make them just funny instead of rather sick-making as they are now."

They bought the play from Joseph Kesselring who agreed that they were to do all the rewriting, but their names were never to appear on the billing except as producers. The first thing they did was change the title to *Arsenic and Old Lace*. The dear old ladies had three nephews—one who was normal and two who were quite mad. One of the mad ones was originally written as a three-hundred-pound man who played with dolls. And one was a sadist who went into a rage when anyone suggested he looked like Boris Karloff. They changed the three-hundred-pounder to a rather adorable man who thought he was Teddy Roosevelt and who yelled "CHARGE!" every time he went bounding up the stairs to take San Juan Hill. They had the brilliant idea of getting their friend Boris Karloff to play the other part. He took a lot of persuading but he finally consented. They changed a great many things from the original script, including the bad smells that came up from the cellar; and they made a lot of other changes from beginning to end. *Arsenic* was a huge success and paid back the backers handsomely.

Howard and Buck (the Beamish Boys, as Boris called them) had great fun in writing letters to the backers when they sent them their checks for the profits. Howard wrote: "Dear Angel: Enclosed you will find our first statement. We think it is a charming document and hope that others more charming will follow. If there is anything in this about which you wish to complain, we will be glad to hear from you. Just address us in care of the Dead Letter Office, Washington, D.C."

Buck wrote the next letter: "Angel dear: Taking advantage of my absence from the city, Howard Lindsay, trying to show off, sent you a check. If Lindsay can give away money I can give away more money, as proved by the enclosed check. Lindsay also enclosed a news bulletin in his letter. All right—if you want news, I can give it to you. We have a Chicago company in rehearsal with Erich Von Stroheim in the lead. We wanted Al Capone but couldn't afford to pay his back taxes. I might add, we are holding two tickets at the Fulton Theatre in the name of Adolf Hitler. However, wait until he sits in them. You need not reply to this letter, but if it comes to our ears that you have any objections to the way this office is being operated, we will be glad to send you free of charge one bottle of Aunt Martha's elderberry wine. P.S. We hope to have companies in Berlin, Rome, and Tokyo this time next year, all playing under the American Flag."

Howard wrote: "Dear Limited Partner: You have been limited by Crouse long enough so I am sending along the enclosed check. This, I hope, will demonstrate to you that so far as the firm of Lindsay and Crouse goes, it is Lindsay who fights on the side of the angels."

Buck wrote: "Dear Angie Wangie: You may breathe easier. Open-hearted Crouse, the backers' boyfriend, has managed to get hold of the checkbook again, and if I can keep Lindsay out of the office for a few minutes, I'll see that you really get a check."

Howard wrote: "Dear Friend: Enclosed is a check for a good round figure. Hoping yours is the same."

Howard was not only a good actor and a good playwright and a good director, he was also a very good citizen. Over the years these were some of the things to which he gave time and devotion. In 1936, Howard had been largely responsible for the founding of the Dramatists Play Service. It was brought into being with the help of the literary agent Harold Freedman, and the lawyer Alexander Lindey, and the other members of the Dramatists Guild. Although the Play Service was set up to handle only amateur rights, it became a vital part of the American theatre. Howard gave willingly of his time to the project. He was its president from its inception for the rest of his life.

Here is part of a letter from Alexander Lindey. The complete letter is framed in gilt and hangs on our library wall. He said: "Most of us occupy ourselves wholly with the business of earning a living. A very few, like you, can find time, energy and devotion not only to shine professionally but also to make contributions of lasting value to their calling and to society. No one knows better than I the long hours, the thought, the balanced judgment and the inexhaustible patience that you have given the Play Service." Signed: "A salute from A.L."

At various times he was president of the Authors League, president of the New Dramatists Committee, vice-president of the Dramatists Guild, chairman of the National Committee on Arts and Government, honorary chairman of the National Committee on Arts and Government, adviser to the New York State Council on the Arts. He was also vice-chairman of the Committee for Modern Courts. And what, I am sure, gave him the greatest pleasure of all, he was president of The Players Club from 1955 to 1965, when he resigned.

At the time he was elected president he agreed to serve for ten years, which he did. He was an enthusiastic Player who dearly loved his club. The presidency brought him great satisfaction as well as a lot of very hard work. The club had grown rather shabby with the years; Howard was one of the men most responsible for restoring it to its original elegance.

Something that was very important to Howard, and very dear to his heart, was the New Dramatists Committee. In 1949, Michaela O'Harra, a young playwright, conceived the plan and brought it to Howard. He and Michaela, with the help of many professionals, made the idea work. It was an organization for developing playwrights who needed to test their skills before offering their plays to producers. A group that gave young playwrights an opportunity to learn more about their craft by discussing their plays and talking to some of the more experienced people of the theatre. Howard got playwrights, producers, directors, scene designers, and other theatre craftsmen to talk to the young playwrights of practical matters, to answer questions, and to give counsel and encouragement. Successful craftsmen who came to talk included

Robert Sherwood, Moss Hart, Richard Rodgers, and Oscar Hammerstein to discuss playwriting; and people such as John Golden, Jo Mielziner, and Joshua Logan to discuss producing, scene designing, and directing.

The list of playwrights who started with the New Dramatists Committee is impressive. To name only a few: Robert Anderson who wrote *Tea and Sympathy*, William Inge who wrote *Picnic*, Paddy Chayefsky who wrote *The Tenth Man*, Michael Stewart who wrote *Hello, Dolly*, and James Goldman who wrote *Lion in Winter*. These are only a few of the many good plays these men have written, and there is a list of over two hundred of the people who started with the New Dramatists and have had their plays produced. The whole thing started with a group of people sitting around a large table to talk. There were never fees for membership. Through the years the New Dramatists has flourished. They now have their own building that is well equipped with a theatre, conference rooms, writing rooms, pianos, and a rehearsal hall available to members the year round. The dream of Michaela O'Harra and Howard Lindsay has come true in a very important and constructive way.

During the *Life With Father* years Lindsay and Crouse had an office at the very top of the Empire Theatre Building. It was arrived at by a shaky little elevator. Running their rooftop office was Anna Erskine, the daughter of John Erskine. She was their secretary as well as their general helper-outer, and she was a darling in every way.

Alison had died of a brain tumor in 1943 and had left Crouse a very lonely man. He and Anna fell blissfully in love and were married sometime later. It was a perfect marriage, and eventually Timothy and Lindsay Ann were born. She was named Lindsay Ann Crouse, as Buck explained, to keep the firm's name alive.

At one time we had become part owners of the Hudson Theatre. The other owners were Peggy and Howard Cullman, Norma and Elliott Nugent, Anna and Russel Crouse, Maggie and Leland Hayward. It is a very strange feeling to own a theatre. One night we were watching a rehearsal of

The Hasty Heart there when Howard started to light a cigarette. He looked guiltily for a fireman who would tell him to put it out, when he realized "This is my theatre. I can smoke if I want to." When we left it was a very strange feeling to lock the front door after us. We really did own a theatre. We kept it for several years before it was sold. *The Hasty Heart, State of the Union,* and *Detective Story* all played there.

Howard and Buck wrote *Strip for Action* while we were in *Life With Father.* It was about a burlesque company who, through a mistake, had been sent to an army camp to entertain the troops. It was cast with burlesque actors and it gave us a great excuse to see a lot of burlesque shows, and they were wonderful. The play had some very funny scenes, but it didn't add up to a success and it soon closed. After that Lindsay and Crouse produced a beautiful play by John Patrick called *The Hasty Heart,* about a young Scottish soldier who comes to a hospital behind the lines with a fatal illness. He is embittered and unpleasant, but is finally won over by the other patients in the ward. The play was touching and funny too.

State of the Union opened in 1945 at the Hudson Theatre with a cast that included Ralph Bellamy, Minor Watson, Ruth Hussey, and Myron McCormick. Burns Mantle wrote of it this way: "It is a story of a search for a liberal—but not too liberal candidate for the presidency to head the Republican Party in 1948. To combine politics and romance in the same comedy is a good trick if you can do it. Few playwrights have been able to turn that trick. As it turned out, *State of the Union* became a very human domestic comedy in which the dramatists' basic impulses were swayed by both their love of laughter and their love of country. The comedy is a tribute to the Lindsay and Crouse playwriting skill and to the keenness of their observation of the American character."

George Jean Nathan summed up the story this way: "Grant Matthews, the man who enters politics with high ideals, who finds that self-seeking politicians would use him to their own ends and who heroically tells them off and goes his independent way, along with the counterpoint of a wife whom his activities have brought him to neglect. The other woman, with whom he has become entangled, and his final discovery after his wife has proved her mettle in public affairs, that it is she whom he has loved all along."

One line was changed every night. When Grant Matthews picks up the day's paper and reads the headline to Mary, the headline was decided upon by seven o'clock every night, and when Mr. Bellamy arrived at the theatre he was told what line to read, and it was always a headline from the newspaper of that very day.

The play was an enormous hit and it won the Pulitzer Prize. Nichols, of the *Times*, said of it: "Wins by a landslide. A good play, perfectly cast, with wonderfully funny lines and situations." Garland, of the *Journal-American*, wrote: "The smash hit for which the theatrical season has been waiting. A very funny, very serious, very welcome play." Rascoe of the *World-Telegram*—"Witty, wise and bright, a satire of the most devastating kind." Chapman of the *News:* "An adult, witty play." Barnes of the *Herald Tribune:* "'State of the Union' speaks out loud about things that need stating. A shining show, eloquent and engaging. A happy combination of wit and sense." Kronenberger of *PM* wrote: "Gets something said that greatly needs to be said."

After Pearl Harbor the war came to our doorstep. Our two eldest "sons," Jack Devereaux and Dick Simon, enlisted. During those depressing times, when the war news was so grim, we were increasingly grateful to be playing in a comedy and to be given the opportunity of making people laugh and at least temporarily forget their anxieties. Two rows of seats were put aside every night at the Empire for the men in service.

It has been said that "Life gives us moments, and for these moments we give our lives." We have all had our moments to hoard—a certain time, a certain place, a certain event that was uniquely ours. Certain scenes that we remember with a smile— times when we were not only happy but when we were vividly aware of our happiness. I remember a hot summer night when we were walking home after a performance. We stopped in front of Lord & Taylor's to watch the men changing the window decorations for the next day. When one of the men turned around we applauded. Then they all looked at us on the sidewalk and applauded in return.

I remember one Sunday during the war when a man from the British Navy had dined with us. Howard had had to keep an appointment at The Players after dinner. It was a foggy night, the Englishman was a stranger to me and to New York, so I suggested a walk. I wanted to show him how beautiful our city looks in the mist. We stopped in at the Church of the Ascension on the corner of Tenth Street and Fifth. It was lighted and entirely empty except for the sexton. My uniformed guest asked and was given permission to play the beautiful organ. I had not known that in civilian life he was an organist and a fine composer. For over an hour he played and improvised while his rapt and astonished audience of one sat in a pew and listened.

I remember the grand feeling when we finished our performance on Saturday night and knew that we had done a good week's work and that we could look forward to Sunday. Sometimes we were driven to the farm on Saturday night. The car would be waiting at the stage door. We would hurry out of our costumes and wigs and wouldn't even wait to take the makeup off. In the car would be a thermos of martinis, a thermos of tea, and a box of sandwiches. About halfway there we would pour the martinis while we sat relaxed and happy in the back seat singing "The Surrey With the Fringe on Top." When we got to the farm we would turn on the music box and have our tea and sandwiches in front of the fire if it was cold; or if it was warm, we would open all the doors to let the smell of honeysuckle come in.

At Christmastime we always put aside one night to cover the town looking at all the beautiful window decorations. One night we stood in front of Schrafft's brightly lighted window resplendent with candies and beautifully decorated cakes. We saw a little mouse running around from cake to cake to candy taking a nibble here and a nibble there. The mouse was having a fine Christmas feast. We stood and laughed, and gradually a crowd gathered to laugh too, and to cheer on the little mouse in his Christmas celebration.

As time went on we became very possessive about the Empire. It was our home, with an actual feeling of permanence about it. We lived there. And it was a very happy family kind of life. We celebrated birthdays and Christmases, and once a year, always, the big party on the anniversary of our opening. People often asked us if we didn't get tired playing the same parts, saying the same words year after year. The answer was a definite "Never." Perhaps that was because it was a comedy and the audience gave us back so much in laughter and joy. We were never bored in the theatre. But I must confess that sometimes our life outside the theatre got very dull and routine. Dinner at six every night. At six-thirty a half-hour's rest. Then to the theatre. Once in a while we would go to Sardi's or Toots Shor's, or the Stork Club for our late supper. More often we came home, had some food and read. We seldom had a chance to see any people outside our own profession. We tried very hard and very consciously to keep our performances fresh. When we felt any staleness creeping in we would ask Bretaigne Windust (Windy, to us) to give us a rehearsal. Our effort was to try to forget we were playing comedy and get back to honesty. Then, too, since our two younger sons grew so fast and had to be replaced, this meant more rehearsals which we were glad of.

We were given two weeks' vacation the first year, while other actors played our parts. After that it was four weeks every summer. On our first vacation we decided to go somewhere we had never been before. We took the car and drove down to the Blue Ridge Mountains. From the company we had a going-away present that was especially made for us. It was a Claxton horn for the car, and it played the first seven notes of "Every Daisy in the Dell." It brought people to the doors of their cabins when we passed through villages. Our first night was spent in Asheville. Of course we phoned New York to see how things were going, secretly hoping that we were missed. The company manager, Walter Fried, told us everything was fine—that there had been twenty-three standees that night. When the receiver was hung up Howard immediately called Walter back and shouted incredulously, "TWENTY-THREE!!"—and hung up.

We had a wonderful stage manager named Van Buren. In his younger days he had been a matinee idol in the stock-company years. He was very strict. He had great respect for the theatre and he taught the little boys to respect it too. A whole generation must have grown up with good theatre manners bred in them. Our wardrobe mistress was a darling Mrs. Malaprop. She said of one of the stagehands: "Oh, don't mind him. He's a pestamist." One day she came in and announced that it was "raining tyrants." She also "took it in her strive," and kept her "nose to the grimstone."

When we were in about our fourth year a friend of mine happened to be standing in the lobby when she overheard a conversation between two old ladies. They had bought their tickets and were killing time by examining the photographs of the people who had played the Empire down through the years since it opened in 1893. One was heard to say to the other, "And to think that all these actresses have played in *Life With Father*." Then they came to the photograph of me, and the other one said: "Yes. But that was the original."

The proudest moment of my life came when my portrait in the character of Vinnie was hung in the inner lobby between Otis Skinner and Margaret Anglin. It had been painted by John Falter and it shows me in the lovely white dress backstage just about to make an entrance. The lighting in the picture is pure theatre. It could not possibly be mistaken for the north light of an artist's studio. John Falter went to great pains to get that particular light effect. It was unmistakably a picture of an actress in the theatre. He had made his preliminary sketches and snapshots backstage. He got the same theatre lights with the same colored gelatins that we used at the Empire. He fitted his studio with them, pulled down the shades, and painted his picture with the theatre lights.

Another vivid memory concerns my treasured friend Willa Frederic, who was first an actress, then a playwright, then one of the editors on *Town and Country* magazine. On a certain Christmas morning we rode together in the front seat of the top deck of a Fifth Avenue bus. It had snowed the night before and the town was clean and brilliant and sparkling and beautiful. We both remember that morning as though it had happened yesterday.

During the fifth year of our stay at the Empire we got the tragic news that the theatre had been sold and in a few years would be torn down to make way for a huge office building. We were shocked and heartbroken.

After *State of the Union*, Howard and Buck had written *Life With Mother* which had been contracted for by Oscar Serlin during the run of *Life With Father*. It was an adorable play about the same Day family plus two wonderful new characters. One was Bessie, which they had written especially for Gladys Hurlbut and she gave the perfect performance of the part.

The play got glowing reviews, even better than the *Life With Father* ones had been, and we were back in our beloved Empire Theatre playing our dear familiar characters again. It ran in New York for only one year, then we took it on the road and closed it after a week. It had been a mistake to call it *Life With Mother*. People must have been subconsciously thinking that it would be *Life With Father* all over again, which they had already seen. We should have called it *The Engagement Ring* which was what it was about.

After that, *The Time of the Cuckoo* played the Empire and the Sunday before that play closed was the sixtieth anniversary of the theatre—January 25, 1893, to January 25, 1953. New York celebrated that anniversary with a gala farewell performance. The cast was made up of actors and actresses who had played there. We had all come back to say a last good-bye to New York's most beautiful theatre which had been hallowed ground for actors.

All the newspapers carried stories about this good-bye. The *Times* headlined their feature article: "END OF THE RUN FOR THE EMPIRE." "A venerable theatre is soon to be torn down but its ghosts and glory will linger." The pictures they printed were scenes from the plays that had been at the Empire through its sixty years. There was a picture from *Rosemary* with Maude Adams, in 1896; one from *Dear Brutus*, with William Gillette and a little girl named Helen Hayes, in 1913; there was Ethel Barrymore in *The Twelve-Pound Look*, in 1911, John Drew and Billie Burke in *My Wife*, in 1917, Katharine Cornell in *The Barretts of Wimpole Street*, in 1931, and Howard Lindsay and Dorothy Stickney in *Life With Father*, in 1939.

The *Times* article continued: "Within a year the Empire Theatre will be rubble. Its hallowed walls will be battered down so that a skyscraper trumpeting the triumph of commerce may be reared on its site. Outraged at the blasphemy, Broadway romantics are already crying into their beer, or if profitably employed, their vintage cups. A classic wake is brewing, for the Empire is both a shrine and a symbol to those who recall the Golden Age of our theatre. An age which reckoned not of movies, talkies, radio and television, and other mechanical intruders, for of all the theatres on Manhattan Island it is the only survivor of the 19th century still devoted to the spoken word. There, John Drew reigned for twenty years in thirty plays, in one of which, 'The Bauble Shop,' in 1894, his fifteen-year-old niece Ethel Barrymore faced her first audience.

"Over the first twenty years Maude Adams, ethereal and aloof, was a constant communicant. It was there that she reached stardom in 'The Little Minister,' in 1897, and there that she played 'Peter Pan,' in 1905. It was there that William Gillette first played 'Sherlock Holmes.' It was in this historic theatre that 'Life With Father' played for eight years, the longest run ever enjoyed by any play anywhere.

"The Empire was built for Charles Frohman by Al Hyman, Fred Sanger, and William Harris. Hyman believed that the amusement sector was edging northward. He had empty lots at Broadway and 40th Street. So great was his confidence in Frohman that he built him a theatre and turned it over to him without the formality of a contract.

"Charles Frohman's enterprises prospered until his death on the *Lusitania* in 1915. Thereafter, the Empire had several operators. It was eventually sold to the William Waldorf Astor Estate. The Empire's knell was sounded when the Astor heirs gave a 99-year lease to the firm that plots the aforementioned skyscraper."

The *World Telegram* headlined its piece: "EMPIRE BOWS OUT AMID CHEERS AND TEARS." "Edna Wallace Hopper returned to do a scene from 'The Girl I Left Behind Me,' the play that opened the Empire in 1893. Star of stars was Cornelia Otis Skinner. With grace, beauty and wit she introduced the numbers, gave the show some of its biggest laughs, and respected its sentiment without ever letting it bog down into bathos. The audience left no doubt that it would just as soon Howard Lindsay and Dorothy Stickney start another five- or ten-year run in 'Life With Father.' They were adored."

John Chapman wrote: "The people who love the theatre most and best of all, the actors, held a grand wake for the Empire Theatre last evening. Everybody must know by now that the sun is setting on the Empire to make room for an office building. Edna Wallace Hopper won a tremendous ovation from the audience after her portrayal of a scene from the Empire's first play, 'The Girl I Left Behind Me,' during which she skipped across the stage like a schoolgirl and coyly impersonated the sunbonneted coquette."

A quote from *Variety* reads: "Basil Rathbone bade official adieu to Charles Frohman's shrine for the spoken word with the lines of Prospero in Shakespeare's *The Tempest*:

"Our revels now are ended.
These our actors, as I foretold you,
Were all spirits and are melted into thin air . . .
We are such stuff as dreams are made on,
And our little life is rounded with a sleep."

Buck and Anna Crouse had a handsome album made for us. They had had a fine photographer take pictures of the Empire from every conceivable view. They were all pasted in the album, ending with a picture of an empty stage with only a pilot light on. In gilt letters on the beautiful red-leather cover it says: "Empire Theatre 1893 to 1953."

Two of the audience seats with "E" on their backs and wire holders for gentlemen's hats underneath their seats were given to us, as well as two of the chairs from a box. They still reside in our front hallway.

A week after the "Farewell to the Empire" show had taken place, and the night before they started tearing down the theatre, that Sunday night before the demolition actually began, when the men would come in the next morning with their pickaxes and start ripping out the seats and pulling down the beautiful proscenium arch, Howard and I took the station wagon and went to collect the painting of me which hung in the inner lobby. We wanted to leave it there as long as there was any Empire Theatre to leave it in. When we arrived it was late Sunday night. A doorman was on duty to guard against vandalism. He let us in. We walked out onto the empty stage and found that the whole theatre was lighted—it was simply ablaze with light and all crimson and gold the way we wanted always to remember it. And the curious thing was that there was not another soul there. We were all alone in that beautiful theatre for our private good-bye—except perhaps for some ghosts in the shadows, perhaps Charles Frohman and Maude Adams might have been there saying good-bye to it too.

I fell in love with Edna St. Vincent Millay when I first came across her poetry in an anthology. I bought her books as fast as they came out, beginning with *A Few Figs From Thistles* and ending with her last published poems, a book called *The Buck in the Snow*. Surely she was speaking for hundreds of small-town boys and girls like me when she wrote: "There isn't a train I wouldn't take no matter where it's going." Two years after her death I read the collection of her letters. It was compiled and edited by Allan Ross Macdougall with the help of Norma Millay, her sister. It was a fascinating book, beginning with a childhood letter to her mother and ending with a note that was written at five-thirty in the morning on the day of her death. It was left for a woman who was coming that day to do the laundry. It cautioned her about a faulty electric iron and ended with the words "Good Morning." These letters were mostly written to people she loved, and occasionally to someone she didn't. They made wonderful reading—so open and outgoing, so revealing that it was like a good biography. The letters gave a picture of a fascinating woman—a gay, warm, and courageous person. I thought there must be some way of putting her story in terms of the theatre, using both poems and letters and juxtaposing them in a way that would add up to the story of her life. I wrote to her sister, Norma, who owns the rights to all the material, to ask if I might try to put it together for the theatre. She gave me her permission but could make no commitment until she saw the finished work.

I made a sort of outline and brought the idea to Paul Gregory who had produced *Don Juan in Hell* with the actors simply sitting on stools and reading their lines. He was most enthusiastic about it and we had some meetings and correspondence, but he finally faded out of the picture. A year or so later I sent the idea to Thornton Wilder, hoping he would want to do it. He wrote me a charming letter which, nevertheless, said he was not interested in the Edna St. Vincent Millay project. I tried to get Paul Osborn to put it together in terms of the theatre but he said no, and explained that it would be a lot of work, and after it was finished it would not belong to him.

I started writing it myself as a rather elaborate production, with two women on the stage to represent her mother as well as her sisters and one man to represent all the men in her life. I thought there should be a screen at the back on which pictures were projected to suggest time and place. This did not work out well. I decided that surely there should be music—Edna St. Vincent Millay was an accomplished pianist—and that occasionally her poems should be done in songs. I finally started to put it together myself. I brought it to Deems Taylor who was a fine composer as well as a music critic. He was intrigued with the idea. He wrote some beautiful music for it, especially for one of the poems called "Dirge"—"Boys and girls who held her dear, do your weeping now." We tried it on an audience of twenty-five people in Emily Kimbrough's drawing room. Emily is a fine writer who has had many books published; the first was *Our Hearts Were Young and Gay,* which she wrote with Cornelia Otis Skinner. Emily's room had two grand pianos, but to my surprise and disappointment the music did not help at all. Every time we stopped for a song the bottom dropped right out of the play, and it had to be picked up off the floor and started over again.

I had never thought of it as a reading, always as a play with three acts and two intermissions. But with music it simply didn't work and Deems recognized the fact as well as I did.

I kept on writing and rewriting and rewriting it, never dreaming that I would be the one to play it. Julie Harris was the actress I had in mind. All this took place over a number of years. Here is an excerpt from my diary of 1956: "I must get to work on Millay. I feel so inadequate. God must show me how to do it myself or else send me someone who will help me."

I would have so welcomed any help from Howard, but it simply was not his cup of tea. This was such a departure from his kind of theatre, there was nothing in his background that related in any way to the kind of thing I was trying to do. I think the idea of one woman alone on a stage talking for nearly two hours seemed to him far too risky. He was probably trying to shield me from disappointment and that is why he backed away every time I brought it up, hoping for his help.

Dick Barr, a distinguished producer who had the courage to do experimental plays, and who is now president of the League of New York Theatres, got very excited about the idea and put together a script himself. Here is an excerpt from my diary of 1957: "I have been going over Dick Barr's last Millay script all evening. I am completely puzzled and baffled and beginning to be sorry I started it—I don't know whether to be stubborn and persistent in trying to put it together, or to give it up entirely. If Howard could help me decide, but he would automatically change the subject again, and his 'noes' have deflated me too many times before when it would have been better if I had gone on trying by myself. I just don't know."

I had a stack of discarded manuscripts a foot high. But the idea of combining her letters and poetry for the stage simply would not let me go. I kept on trying it different ways. It was nearly seven years from the time I first thought of it until it finally reached the stage in 1960. I had put it all together myself with the script being almost entirely in Millay's own words, the words of her poems and of her letters. I kept myself out of it as much as possible, only stepping in when some explanation was needed to keep the performance clear. The Millay material was so very rich that it was never so much a question of what I used as it was of what I could eliminate. One summer on a trip to England I saw my old friend Emlyn Williams and told him what I was trying to do. He gave me most valuable advice. He said, "Dorothy, keep it simple." He told me that when he was first trying out his Dickens show he had Mrs. Dickens and other characters in it and that it never came right until he eliminated everything extraneous—everything except Dickens' own words.

After my talk with Emlyn I threw away all the scripts and started over again. It began to come right. Nothing but Millay's own words except when I had to step in to clarify something. I named the play *A Lovely Light* from her four-line verse—

> My candle burns at both ends
> It will not last the night
> But ah, my foes, and oh, my friends,
> It gives a lovely light.

I had made two trips to Steepletop, the place high in the Berkshire Hills which had been Millay's home for twenty-five years and now was lived in by her sister. Finally the script was finished and I then had to get Norma Millay's permission to use it. I felt as though I was about to audition for a part that I wanted more than anything in the world. I telephoned and asked her to come to New York and let me read it to her. I prayed that she would like it enough for me to go ahead. I was scared to death. She and her husband, Charles Ellis, sat in our living room one night and listened while I read it. I had icy hands and a thumping heart. But after it was over a wonderful thing happened. Norma cried and hugged me and gave her blessing to the project.

I asked Robert Porterfield if I might try it out in his Barter Theatre in Abingdon, Virginia. He booked me for a week.

Howard's attitude had changed. He liked the finished script and did everything he could to help. In the summer of '59, Howard and I went to Abingdon to see if I had something that would work. My treasured friend Gladys Hurlbut and her husband, Charles de la Vergne, drove down to Abingdon to see the performance. She was the first one ever to give me any encouragement. Perhaps I would never have stuck to the project if it had not been for her belief in it. After the opening night there Howard said to Gladys: "I think we have something here. I don't know just what. But something important."

What I did not know was that the Hurok office had sent a representative, Harold Shaw, down from New York to look at it. The day after I opened there was a wire from the Hurok office. It was from Harold Shaw and he told me that he had been haunted all day with the memory of it and that Hurok would like to book me in the show. Of course I was in seventh heaven. Hurok was the most important impresario in the country. Howard turned out to be my best audience. He saw the performance again and again, and always laughed and cried in the right places.

After I had played *A Lovely Light* in Abingdon I wanted more experience to learn how to do it and to make corrections when they were necessary, so I took it to three remote summer theatres for one week in each. I learned that there are certain things necessary for playing in remote summer-stock companies. One might think that the most important things would be your script, your makeup, and your costume, but I learned that the most important things to carry are a fly swatter and a small electric plate for making a cup of tea at intermission. I have a strong phobia against things that flutter or fly, and the fly swatter was no help against birds and bats. During the week in Gettysburg there was a bat that came out on cue every single night and swooped past me. It was while I was sitting on the red sofa in a spotlight and my line was, appropriately enough, ". . . and what evil thing can ever again brush me with its wings?" But in spite of birds and bats and flies, the three weeks did me a great deal of good.

When I came back to New York I had a lovely costume made. It had to be timeless because the play covered her whole life-span, and I wanted it to somehow suggest Millay. Helene Pons made it of very heavy dark blue silk. It was floor length and had a wide belt and a bolero jacket, and white collar and cuffs. It moved beautifully and was very easy to work in.

Howard found a wonderful cabinetmaker for me and he made the three necessary pieces of furniture that I used on the stage. It was all the break-away kind that could be packed in crates for the coast-to-coast tours. There was a red velvet winged-backed loveseat, and there was a beautiful table desk with a blue-leather top, and a small bench that was covered with black velvet so it simply faded into the background of a black curtain until it was necessary to use it.

The Hudson Theatre was available because Lillian Hellman's play *Toys in the Attic*, which had been booked there, was not ready to come in. The theatre seemed to promise good luck since Howard and I were once part owners of it and since *The Hasty Heart* and *State of the Union* had both played there. It had all been refurbished and was beautiful with white walls and crimson curtain and carpet and seats. Curiously enough, in my own show I didn't suffer from stage fright as much as usual. It was bad standing in the wings waiting for it to start and bad for about the first five minutes. After that I wasn't scared and it went wonderfully well. The house was "mouse still," to quote a review, and the audience laughed and cried when I hoped they would. Mobs of people came back afterward, some of them in tears. My flowers were beautiful and there was a wire from Mr. Hurok that said,

"With love." I was delighted to have the Hudson to play in as I wanted so much to have *A Lovely Light* judged by Broadway standards.

Emily Kimbrough gave a party afterward but I was too tired to enjoy it. When Howard and I came home about one o'clock we were sitting at the kitchen table when Walter Alford, who was the press agent, rang the doorbell and came in with the *Times*. He read us the Brooks Atkinson review. It was unbelievably wonderful and so were all the others, which we saw later, including the A.P. and the U.P. and *Variety*. I wouldn't have had the audacity even to dream such good notices. One which I particularly liked called it "an interior biography" which was what I had so hoped it would be. There were more than two hundred letters during the two weeks I played. They were fine letters and only a few among them were the "Dear Miss Stickney, I am your fan, please send me an autographed photograph" kind. Peggy and I answered them all.

If it had not been for Howard none of this might have happened. He gave me no encouragement at all during the years when I was trying to put it together in some form for the stage. But from the time he started liking it he had been just wonderful and helpful in every way. He began believing in it about the time I got the first act ready to try out at The Players Club. He had gotten the Hudson Theatre and he got Walter Alford who did a great job as press agent. I had the front page of the theatre section of the Sunday *Times*, with a picture of Millay and a picture of me. Howard watched me rehearse and was enormously helpful in the staging, besides being my best audience. I played it on TV as one of a series called "Festival of the Performing Arts." It was one of the first things to be done with no commercial interruptions.

I went to Los Angeles to have two wigs made. On the road I simply could not cope with my fine hair while doing one-night stands. In Los Angeles I met Olga Stevens who had answered the ad that I'd put in the *Saturday Review*. She seemed to be exactly the person I was hoping for to accompany me on tour. She had done one-nighters on the road before. It seemed like fate that she was in Los Angeles at the same time I was there. She even drove a car, which was helpful when we couldn't make connections any other way. I grew to love her very much.

My precious friend Fleur Cowles had been a magazine editor, a writer, and a painter whose pictures are shown all over the world. She now lives in London. She interested Hugh Beaumont, the London producer, in my show and he booked me into the Globe Theatre in June. I was not a success and we closed in ten days instead of the two and a half weeks I had been scheduled for. The London *Times* gave it a moderately good review but the tabloids were just terrible. They didn't know me which, of course, I had expected, but they also didn't know Edna St. Vincent Millay which surprised me. There were some nice letters, particularly one from Lynn Fontanne and Alfred Lunt which I treasured. Howard was with me and that made everything better. I discovered I could give as good a performance to a practically empty house as I could to a full one.

After we came back I started a coast-to-coast tour of one-night stands, except for Chicago and Los Angeles where I played a week each. John Wilson, who worked for Hurok, came with me as stage manager, and lovely Olga Stevens came to help me pack up after each performance and to drive a rented car when necessary. After that I did a tour of the South and Middle West without Olga, and with Andy Meyers as stage manager, whose function it was to get the furniture uncrated and set up the stage and to see that I had a lighting rehearsal the day before the performance, if possible, and to drive the car when we needed one.

My sporadic diary records: "I have crossed and recrossed and double crossed the Middle West and South so many times that I know all the Chicago railroad stations intimately and feel pretty much at home in the Cincinnati station too.

"We get where we are going by any means available except on our hands and knees. But even the bad parts have their laughs, in fact, the worse the funnier. Took night train to Kansas City arriving 7:00 A.M., breakfast which was good in

Harvey dining room in station. Train to Shreveport, Louisiana, arriving 10:00 P.M. Wanted a hot bath but water came out black and tub wouldn't drain, so I borrowed a bath from Andy Meyers across the hall. My dressing room contained the only toilet in the house. I couldn't tell whether the ladies who flocked back after the show had come to see me or to go to the toilet. One lady stayed and watched while I undressed and dressed and packed my suitcases.

"Monday noon Buck phoned me that Howard had fainted at a cocktail party and had been taken to Presbyterian Hospital. My heart went to my feet as it has done so many times. If all the prayers I have prayed for Howard were laid end to end they would reach to London and back. I was just about to call Eli Bauman, who had been our friend and our doctor for so many years, when Howard called me from the hospital sounding chipper as could be, and saying he was feeling fine but was staying there for a few days for tests. Then I called the doctor and was assured it was nothing serious. I told him I would walk out on my remaining shows and fly back, but he told me that nothing warranted that."

My diary also records: "I had a lighting rehearsal and dinner at five-thirty in my room, as usual. Andy drove me to the theatre in a rented car. We got lost and arrived late. What with that and worrying about Howard and removing the Christmas decorations from the dressing room to make a place for my makeup I was pretty nervous. After the show we drove 125 miles to Alexandria. I had provided tea and coffee and sandwiches in my trusty picnic bag. (Three things one learns never to travel without—thermos bottles, dressing-room lights, and a flask of bourbon.) It was a clear, cold night. There was a full moon and the road was perfectly straight and traffic-less. The air smelled good. When we stopped to eat we found that the sandwiches were made of soggy and burned toast, but we were hungry. We got to Alexandria about 2:30 A.M. and it was another half hour before we could find the hotel we were booked into. I was put into a fancy room with roaring air conditioning and an overpowering smell of paint. Moved to a smaller, quite dirty room where I could breathe.

Woke the next morning thinking it was raining. It wasn't. The sun was shining brightly but the window was *that* dirty.

"In Pineville the dressing room was a sort of backstage storeroom, with a table so scarred and stained that it looked dirty even after I had washed it. There was a filthy washbasin that ran only hot water. I had to ask for a pitcher of ice water and a basin so that I could cool the water enough to be able to drink it and use it for my makeup.

"Took a day coach out next afternoon. Had dinner of franks and beans out of a can in a little kind of club car which was cozy. Changed to a through train in New Orleans. Left an hour later. There is a record freeze here in the South. Train crawled along all night because the signals were frozen. Lost five hours and missed connections in Atlanta. Waited there from four in the afternoon until ten at night. Wired Buck to tell Howard I would be late. He is to come home from the hospital at 11:00 A.M. the day I get back. I hope he is all right. The tests showed nothing alarming. I shall be so glad to see him and to get a good bath. I am pretty grubby."

Howard wrote this piece for the *Saturday Review*. Here it is:

OUR SECOND HONEYMOON

My wife, Dorothy Stickney, and I met in a summer stock company at Skowhegan, Maine. We played there together for five years. Then the fortunes of the theatre kept us away from Maine, except for the week we tried out "Life With Father," in 1939.

The years following were "Maine-less" until two years ago when the University of Maine, which is at Orono (a fact known to all crossword puzzle-ists), booked Dorothy to do her dramatization of the letters and poems of Edna St. Vincent Millay, "A Lovely Light," at the university. They wanted me to accompany her and give a talk on the theatre. I was glad of this excuse to go with her. We had fallen in love in Maine and been married in Maine. It would be a second honeymoon.

The month was March, and we planned to fly to Bangor, which is next door to Orono, but a heavy snowstorm started the day before so we hurriedly took a train to Boston. When we reached there the storm had become a blizzard. At the North Station we learned there were no passenger trains to Bangor. To our astonishment there were no passenger trains that went beyond Portland, Maine. I bought two tickets for Portland, and wired the Eastland Hotel there for a room overnight. The redcap who took our bags asked us our destination and I told him Portland. He put us in the front coach of the train. It did not occur to me that he had any special reason for doing this.

As the train started I wandered to the door of the coach and to my amazement found myself looking through the falling snow straight up the tracks. There was no engine. From the conductor I learned that we were in something called a Budd car. The locomotion was a diesel engine.

Dorothy and I had spread ourselves over the double seat in the front of the car this side of the washrooms, and were enjoying looking out of the window at the swirling blizzard that was whitening the landscape and beating against the window panes.

About an hour or so after leaving Boston, I started for the washroom. I even got there. I opened the door, closed it immediately and went back to my seat. Part of the campaign on the part of the railroads to discourage passenger service is never to clean the washrooms or care whether or not the plumbing is in order.

After an uncomfortable half hour a simple and intelligent solution occurred to me—I would go back into the coach behind us, which I did, where I found the washroom in the rear end of the coach and not impossible to use. The walk to the car behind was an easy one because the train was at a standstill.

It was not moving when I left the washroom and walked forward to rejoin my wife. To my surprise I found myself again staring out of the window of the door at the front of the coach, into the swirling blizzard on the tracks ahead. I asked a man standing by the door where my coach was. He said, "The Portland coach? There it goes," and pointed to two small red lights disappearing along the tracks into the distance. In a panic I opened the door of the car with the idea of pursuit, but the snow was two feet deep and I decided it would be futile to try to catch up with the Budd car in which was riding my hat, my overcoat, my muffler, my rubbers, and my wife.

I went back inside and asked, "Where is this train going?"

"North Conway, New Hampshire," he told me.

"How can I get from North Conway, New Hampshire, to Portland, Maine?" He had no idea. Then I learned we were now standing in the railroad yards at Dover, New Hampshire. The station of Dover was a few hundred yards ahead but the train didn't stop there. Perhaps it would if I spoke to the conductor and motorman when they arrived.

Dorothy loves riding on trains and can look out the train window watching a snowstorm for hours on end. About twenty minutes after leaving Dover, however, she turned to call my attention to the beauty of it all. My absence didn't alarm her—I must have gone to the men's room. Then, after ten minutes or so, she strolled back through the coach expecting to find me somewhere concentrated on a crossword puzzle. She didn't find me, but she did discover that there were no other coaches except the one in which she was riding.

She asked the conductor to look in the men's room and make sure that I wasn't ill. He reported to her that there was no one in the men's room. She demanded to know where I could be. She wanted an answer and she wanted one right away. The conductor suggested that perhaps I had stepped off the coach to get a breath of fresh air at Dover. But she pointed to my overcoat and muffler, the snowstorm outside, and could only imagine if this were true I was lying somewhere beside the tracks with a broken leg and freezing to death. The train would simply have to go back to Dover where they could search for me. This very reasonable request was refused.

Then she demanded that at the next station they would telephone back to the station at Dover and have a search instituted. She was told the station at Dover could not be reached by telephone. The conductor found he had a mad woman on his hands—mad in the sense of being hysterical and unreasonable, and mad in the sense of being damn angry at the lack of cooperation. He said that at the next stop they would telephone the Boston police, who would telephone the Dover police, and he would check with the Boston police for any news at each station as the train continued to Portland. She sat down and stared at my overcoat and hat and rubbers, and unsuccessfully fought her fantasies of a dying husband, freezing to death in a blizzard.

Meanwhile, back at the North Conway Budd car! I was nervously awaiting the arrival of a conductor and motorman. Most of my fellow passengers were carrying skis. They were chatting away with each other in gay and happy tones. This snowstorm was a stroke of luck.

The motorman reached us first. I explained my predicament. He seemed to think I had been stupid, but he agreed to stop the coach at the Dover Station. Some minutes later a puzzled-looking conductor arrived through the storm. After a glance through the car he came to me and asked, "Are you Mr. Lindsay?" I said I was, and he said, "The Boston police wanted me to find you. They said your wife was worried about you." My explanation of what had happened sounded silly even to me, but he said he would get the Boston police back on the phone and have them telephone ahead to relieve my wife's mind. This took considerable time.

Finally the car started, and stopped at the Dover Station. I had to get through several drifts to make its door. After crossing through the station I found myself on what looked like a main street, and also, to my delight, saw a taxicab coming along it.

I stopped the cab by the simple procedure of getting in front of it, then I jumped into the seat with the driver. I said, "Take me to Portland." He shifted his gears and started, then looked at me with what in the theatre we call a "delayed take."

"Portland, *Maine?*"

I said yes, and again heard myself making the silly explanation. He lifted the speaker of the taxicab's radio and told the dispatcher that he had a passenger who wanted to go to Portland, Maine. The dispatcher's voice came back, "Now? Tonight? In this storm?"

"Yes," and added gamely, "I'm willing. What's the rate?"

"Twenty-five dollars."

"That's fine!" I hurried to say. "Twenty-five dollars is all right."

We started ahead, but he turned off the main road into a side street. The driver explained he had to fill up with gas at a company station. The gas station was dark but he got out and tended to the chore of putting the gas in himself. While he was out of the car the voice of the dispatcher came over the radio, "I wouldn't take anybody to Portland, Maine, on a night like this. I certainly wouldn't take them for twenty-five dollars." I grabbed the speaker and said, "That's all right—I'll pay more." But he couldn't hear me and I didn't know how to make him hear me.

When the driver returned I told him of the dispatcher's conversation and assured him I was perfectly willing to pay more. He got in touch with the dispatcher and it was worked out between them that I should be charged thirty dollars. Little did they know I would have settled for twice that amount.

The driver had to concentrate on his driving and was, as a New Englander, characteristically taciturn. He wanted thirty dollars but he didn't want any conversation along with it. It was a silent ride.

I knew the time Dorothy was due in Portland and added a generous amount to allow her to reach the hotel; then I asked my silent friend to stop at a telephone pay station booth. There were lighted ones, occasionally, along the highway. Unlike the cab, the telephone booth wasn't heated. I got Information at Portland, the number of the Eastland Hotel, and finally the hotel operator who tried to get the desk clerk. It seemed the desk clerk was busy taking care of some arrivals and I had a long wait. I was damned cold. When finally I reached the clerk and gave him my name, he said, "Your wife has just started up to her room. She told me you might get here sometime tonight or tomorrow." I was too chilled to wait to speak to Dorothy. I left word with him to let my wife know I would be there in an hour or so.

When we reached the Eastland Hotel I gave the driver thirty dollars and a five-dollar tip, which was none too generous, but he seemed happy enough with it. His thank-you was brief but for the first time his voice was cordial. I dashed through the snow across the sidewalk and up the steps, and into the welcome warmth of the lobby. When I registered the clerk told me the number of our room and I hurried to the elevator and up to our floor.

I knew Dorothy would be glad to see me, and she was. She embraced me and clung to me, but I couldn't tell whether she was laughing or crying. I felt that the story of my adventures, details such as how cold I was in the telephone booth, would be very interesting to my wife. Do you know, I couldn't quite hold her attention. She wanted me to hear what *she* had been through—her shock at my absence, her fears that I was dead or dying. She seemed to think her experiences had been much more harrowing. I could tell she was upset because it is unlike Dorothy to be selfish. —Howard Lindsay

Lindsay and Crouse produced *Detective Story*, a melodrama by Sidney Kingsley, and they wrote another musical called

Call Me Madam in which Ethel Merman played a friend of President Truman's, who had been appointed as ambassador (ambassadress?) to a small Central European country. She wasn't actually called Perle Mesta but the parallel was there. Irving Berlin wrote great songs for it, including "The Hostess With the Mostest" and "It's a Lovely Day Today," and the duet with Merman and the juvenile Russell Nype, which ended "You're Not Sick, You're Just in Love." *Call Me Madam* was a great big beautiful hit. Ethel looked stunning in her lovely Mainbocher clothes.

A few days after the opening of *Call Me Madam* an old friend, Barbara Wolferman, came to dinner and brought us a present of a little Siamese kitten. She was adorable, light beige with four black paws, a black face, and bright blue eyes. Of course we called her "Madam." Our other cat, all black and named "Friday the Thirteenth," hated her but she wasn't the least bit afraid. She took over the whole household very soon. She was most talkative. In the mornings when my breakfast tray came up she would always start her conversation at the bottom of the stairs and never stop until three flights up when she jumped on my bed, crawled under the breakfast tray and went to sleep. She had the loudest purr of any cat I ever knew. She wouldn't even wait to be petted. If one gave her a compliment such as "Madam, you are a beautiful cat," the motor would start. She was very affectionate and loved to lie in laps. Once she climbed up the dining-room curtain and I had to use a stepladder to get her down. She loved riding in the car with us. When she saw us getting ready to leave for the country she would go and sit in her traveling box making sure she would not be left behind. She would sleep all the way to the farm or sit looking out the back window. Whenever we stopped to pay a toll she gave a great growl. She also loved to curl up in a large ruby glass bowl that was kept on the sideboard. She was a completely enchanting thing. We loved her dearly and she loved us right back. She lived to be seventeen years old. I have had other cats since then, but none can compare with Madam. I still miss her.

There was *Kind Sir* in 1953 with Mary Martin (this was her

first nonmusical), Charles Boyer, Margalo Gillmore, Bob Ross (her husband), Frank Conroy, and me. It was produced and directed by Joshua Logan which meant that he was in complete control of everything. What made it all so frightening was that Josh was in the most manic stage of his manic depression. While we were rehearsing in New York it seemed to me that Josh often had a handful of yellow sleeping pills which he seemed to be eating like candy.

At our last New York rehearsal before opening in New Orleans the play was running three hours long. Josh would not permit anything to be cut or speeded up. We all realized he was in bad shape, but there didn't seem to be anything we could do about it. Sometimes he would yell directions from the back of the theatre in a really outrageous way. We never knew what to expect of him, and it was a nightmarish kind of feeling.

When we got to New Orleans on the afternoon of the night we were to open, Josh and Norman Krasna, who was the author of the play, assembled the cast in a hotel room and cut forty-five minutes out of the play which, of course, made everyone very insecure. That night when the company was standing in the wings waiting for the curtain to go up, Josh was making a speech to the audience to assure them that this was a comedy and that they mustn't be afraid to laugh. The speech went on forever, while we, waiting just offstage, were dying of frustration. We got through the performance somehow. Luckily we were all old friends and also old friends of Josh's, and we managed to come through some bad times by leaning on each other.

Josh was one of my treasured friends and I loved him dearly, but at this point I was afraid of him and afraid for him too. Rumors kept coming back to us from New York that the play was in trouble. We stoutly denied that anything was wrong. Josh was in a hospital before we opened in New York. He is completely cured now, and he remembers very little of what went on with the play during those very bad days on the road. *Kind Sir* had a moderately good run, but we were all relieved when it closed.

In 1955, I played in *The Honeys*, a macabre comedy by

Roald Dahl, with Jessica Tandy and Hume Cronyn. It lasted a very short season.

In the years that intervened between my first try at putting the Millay story in some dramatic form, way back in 1953 to the time it finally opened in New York in 1960, I had done a few pictures. One called *The Catered Affair* with Bette Davis and Ernest Borgnine, and Barry Fitzgerald and Debbie Reynolds. I also did three plays. *To Be Continued*, a charming play by William Marchant, which lasted only a few weeks. Luella Gear and Jean Dixon were in the cast, as well as a pretty little ingenue named Grace Kelly. It was her first Broadway show. She is now Her Serene Highness Princess Grace of Monaco.

Lindsay and Crouse did *Remains To Be Seen*, a mystery drama, and *The Prescott Proposals*, with a political background and with Katharine Cornell as the star.

But the play that was the biggest success and the most fun for all of us was written for Alfred Lunt and Lynn Fontanne. Lynn had told them that she had always wanted to play a cockney, so they wrote *The Great Sebastians*. It concerned a vaudeville team who did a fake mind-reading act. They are playing in Prague, Czechoslovakia, just after it has been taken over by the Communists. They get mixed up with the Russian Secret Police after they have boasted they know Jan Masaryk and had recently had lunch with him. While they are in the company of the Secret Police they learn that Jan Masaryk has committed suicide. They are arrested and escape just in the nick of time. It was a very funny and exciting play. In my opinion one of the best ever written by the Beamish Boys. Of course Lunt and Fontanne were magnificent.

Happy Hunting was another musical for Ethel Merman, and *Tall Story* was about a basketball team. In 1956, my diary records this: "Howard and Buck are going to do a musical called *Happy Hunting* for Ethel Merman and directed by Abe Burrows. I am sorry—this is the first time I have ever not liked one of their shows, but I don't like the outline of this one. I am afraid they will be accused of doing a rehash of *Call Me Madam*. I am probably wrong and this will probably turn out to be their biggest hit." It didn't.

While I was trying out my one-woman show in summer-stock companies, Oscar Hammerstein and Dick Rodgers and Howard and Buck had almost finished doing *The Sound of Music*. The original idea had come from Mary Martin. I got back from my summer tour just in time to see the dress rehearsals. The play was based on a true story of the Von Trapp family when they lived in Austria. Some years later they became known to American audiences as "The Von Trapp Family of Singers." There were the Mother (the Baroness) and seven children, all with beautiful voices. They had eventually come here to sing in concert after they had escaped the Hitler regime.

The play takes place at a much earlier period of their lives. Mary Martin played a young postulate in a convent near the estate of the Baron Von Trapp. She had been sent by the convent to look after the seven children of the Baron. Maria loves the children dearly. They sing and romp together. Maria and the Baron fall in love and are married. They narrowly escape being captured by the Nazis by walking at night over the mountains into Italy.

The musical was beautifully done and the combination of Rodgers and Hammerstein and Lindsay and Crouse was a most happy collaboration.

The Sound of Music was a terrific hit except with the critics who panned it. They accused it of being too sweet and sentimental. Nobody liked it but the audiences, and they flocked to it night after night. It had a run of 1,443 performances, or nearly five years.

There was one thing that saddened us all immeasurably. During the Boston run Oscar Hammerstein was in a hospital there. He was to die of cancer a few months later. One day after he went into the hospital he sent Mary Martin a new song, and that night Mary sang for the first time—

> "A bell is no bell till you ring it
> A song is no song till you sing it
> And love wasn't put in your heart just to stay
> Love isn't love till you give it away."

She gave a fine performance as did Theodore Bikel playing the Baron Von Trapp who was a navy captain and a widower with seven children. The children were adorable on the stage. The sisters of the convent had been cast for their operatic voices; they also had operatic physical proportions. Howard and Buck referred to them as the "Bull Nuns."

Sound of Music was also a tremendous hit in London where it played the Palace Theatre and broke all long-run records there. When it was done as a picture it broke all records again. A longer run than *Gone With the Wind*. *Jaws* has now outdistanced it by a narrow margin. The New York *Times* wrote of *Sound of Music*: "Biggest money-making picture of all time," and added, "How come?" Howard wrote a letter in reply, which was printed in the *Times Magazine*. It said:

> To the Editor:
>
> Through long experience I have learned that a play in the theatre is one thing, and that a motion picture is something else. They are two different art forms.
>
> The fantastic success of the picture of "The Sound of Music" must be credited to Robert Wise, producer and director, and scriptwriter Ernest Lehman. It was a success in the theatre but it could easily have been made into a failure as a motion picture. Joan Barthel's article "Biggest Money-Making Picture of All Time—How Come?" (Nov. 20) recalls to my mind a story about Maurice Barrymore, the father of all the Barrymores. Playing billiards one day at The Players, he made an extraordinarily successful shot. A profane onlooker exclaimed, "Holy God!" "No," murmured Barrymore, "no, not wholly God. I had a hand in it myself."
>
> Much has been written of the success of "The Sound of Music" play and motion picture. Is it immodest of me to point out, because no one else *ever* does, that Russel Crouse and I had a hand in it?

It was a most happy collaboration between Dick and Oscar and Howard and Buck. They all liked each other and worked beautifully together. Dick Rodgers wrote to me one time saying: "What makes me happy about the way the show has been behaving through these years is that you and Anna are so pleased with it. It has been wonderful for all of us, and you both must feel very proud of Howard and Buck. I am sure I have told you that our association was one of the happiest experiences of my theatrical life."

A much less happy experience came the year that Lindsay and Crouse wrote *Mr. President*. That summer Howard and I had stayed in a hotel in Annisquam, a village on Cape Ann, where the Crouses had their summer home. The boys wrote *Mr. President* there. Leland Hayward produced it, Irving Berlin wrote the songs, and Josh Logan directed it. It sounded like the perfect combination of talents. The play had a tremendous advance sale, but by the time it went into rehearsal both Howard and Buck were sick. Buck was recovering from a heart attack and Howard seemed terribly weak and had to spend a lot of time in bed. They were not well enough to take an active part in the preparations, and the play went into rehearsal not quite ready. It was about an honest and attractive President who, during the last four months of his term in office, is longing to return to his Midwestern hometown. His lovely wife is also homesick. His daughter is a pretty girl who is pursued by beaux. His son has studied the Russian language in college and is able to put it to good use when an international crisis occurs. Walter Kerr said of it: "It is always painful when a man you admire introduces you to his awkward and charmless fiancée. What, do you think, he sees in her? 'Mr. President' is awash with people you admire . . . but there is nothing, alas nothing, to win us over." In spite of its terrific advance sale the show was a failure and lasted only 225 performances. This was the last thing that Howard and Buck were ever to write together.

But I have gotten miles ahead of myself talking about the various plays up through *Sound of Music* and *Mr. President*.

Howard and I had lived in our house on Eleventh Street for eighteen years before moving to Ninety-fourth Street. My memories of those years in the Village are as vivid and as random as those snapshots you never quite get around to sorting out and pasting in an album. I remember joining the carol singers in Washington Square on Christmas Eve—"Joy to the

World!"—and remember thinking of the Germans who were certainly not singing even their own carols on this wartime Christmas—I remember creeping downstairs at three in the morning to raid the refrigerator—finding Howard there for the same purpose—deciding to listen to those new phonograph records again—deciding that it was too late to go to bed anyway, so why not take a walk and watch it get daylight—having our neighbors in the block drop in unexpectedly—"We saw your lights on"—what a lovely cozy thing to do—those happy, hardworking years of *Life With Father*—coming home at night tired but satisfied, sitting in the dark garden to listen to the rustle of our poplar tree and to let ourselves unwind. Or in winter lighting a fire and reading aloud for an hour or so before going to bed. I remember spring with the Villagers planting their window boxes with flowers from the vendor's cart—I remember taking a walk alone at night after a snowfall, returning home walking in my own tracks, the only footprints in the street-lighted snow—I loved to ride the Sixth Avenue elevated high in the air, or to walk under its plaid shadow on the street.

Shortly after Howard and I were married came a bad period with my eyes and with it came the joyous discovery that not only did Howard love to read aloud but that he did it beautifully. Also, that we liked and disliked the same kind of books. Reading together has been a very important part of our marriage—sharing a book, like anything else, with someone you love adds a value, a luster to the experience. The first book Howard and I read together was *Of Human Bondage*. What a vivid memory that is. Howard by the big lamp, me on the couch in the shadow listening. When it became evident what pain and heartbreak were in store for the character we loved at the hands of the character *he* loved but *we* hated, it was too much to bear. I said, "Howard, you'll have to stop. I can't stand it." He said, "I can't either. It's awful." We looked at each other and laughed at our lack of courage and said, "What shall we do now?" The one thing we couldn't do was to put the book down, so we decided to have a drink. We did. We had several. We were able to finish the book and we had

had a splendid time. We shared the beauty of *How Green Was My Valley*—the excitement and horror of *The Turn of the Screw* and *The Innocent Voyage*—the fun of *The Crock of Gold* and *The Return of the Hero*—the romance and loveliness of *Precious Bane*. After our performance at the theatre one night we started *The Lost Weekend* and finished it by broad daylight, and of course most important of all, we had laughed together over Clarence Day's *Life With Father* stories in *The New Yorker*. During all the years of our marriage many wonderful things have happened to us, but we both have agreed that nothing has given us more content, a warmer, cozier, more close-together feeling than closing our door, settling down comfortably and picking up "our book."

One night when we were walking around in Washington Square we passed a drunken derelict stretched out on one of the benches fast asleep. We put a ten-dollar bill in his hand just for the fun of imagining how bewildered and surprised he would be when he woke up and found it there.

We loved riding in Central Park in hansom cabs. I remember one particular night. It was very hot and a weekend, and almost everybody had left town. We felt that the park was our private property. I wrote some verses about it.

> By way of the park on a misty night
> We enter the country of heart's delight;
> Away from realities dross and drab
> My love and I in a hansom cab.
>
> The clock in a neighboring tower shows two,
> The hurrying cars in the park are few,
> So we jog along on our hansom throne,
> The king and queen of a land our own.
>
> We're out from under the city's roofs.
> The soothing rhythm of horse's hoofs
> Are beating a song on the asphalt wet
> That curves like a river of gleaming jet.
>
> And stretching away on either hand
> Are lighted vistas of fairyland.
> Against the sky is a castle tall
> A glamour and glory has touched it all.

With Howard in *Life With Mother* (COURTESY *Vogue* MAGAZINE. COPY-
RIGHT © 1948, 1976 BY THE CONDÉ NAST PUBLICATIONS INC.)

A scene from *Life With Mother* (PHOTOGRAPH BY VANDAMM)

One of the *Life With Father* anniversary parties. From left, Mary Martin, John Patrick, me, and John Van Druten (PHOTO BY COSMO-SILEO)

Another party picture with, from left, Oscar Serlin, Russel Crouse, Howard, and me (PHOTO BY COSMO-SILEO)

Yet another birthday party with, from left, me, Helen Hayes, and Gypsy Rose Lee (PHOTO BY COSMO-SILEO)

Howard and Buck at work (ELINOR MAYER)

MEN AT WORK

Men at work in Annisquam (DOROTHY STICKNEY)

oward and me on the *Queen Mary*

A Lovely Light, a dramatization of the
ters and poems of Edna St. Vincent Millay

In *Pippin* (PHOTOGRAPH BY MARTHA SWOPE)

We talk a little of that and this,
We hum a tune and we lean to kiss,
And laugh that a man in a taxi stares
At love's-young-dream-in-a-cab, who cares?

So hand in hand in a sweet content
We drive and drive till the money's spent,
Then we drive toward home when it's half-past three
The horse is sleepy and so are we.

We went to London and to Paris occasionally. Paris, that beautiful city where one is always aware of the lovely sky. London that is bronze and brown and red and soft, but New York that vertical city is hard and sparkling and exhilarating, it is silver and gray and platinum and diamonds.

Marriages often develop a kind of private language. Here is a piece that Howard wrote for the *Saturday Review*.

MR. AND/OR MRS. LINDSAY REGRET

There are two sayings my wife and I have found so useful as shortcuts in communication that I would like to pass them along. Both were originally lines spoken from the stage. The first one was used by a monologist years ago who told of seeing a cat in the topmost branches of a tree. He climbed the tree to rescue the poor thing. When he reached the cat, it turned out to be a wildcat. His only hint of what followed was to say, "I never got so tired of one animal in all my life."

The other phrase came from a comic named Harry Kelly, who was usually called "The Deacon." He wore a Prince Albert, a high hat, and a sorrowful expression. In a restaurant scene the waiter approached his table and asked, "Are you enjoying your soup?" Kelly did not give him a direct answer. He just turned his sad eyes to the waiter and said, "I'm sorry I stirred it."

So whenever Dorothy tells me of something she has been through and says, "I never got so tired of one animal —" I know just how she feels. And when I report to her about some activity in which I got myself involved and

say, "I'm sorry I stirred it," she knows at once the depth
of my despair and regret.

Howard Lindsay

Another line that only we understood came from way back
in Dickinson. Our priest was very Irish. One Sunday he told
about how Jesus raised Lazarus from the dead. He said: "Jesus
looked down on Lazarus who had been dead three days and
you could smell him a mile. Jesus said, 'Lazarus, get up out of
that.' " This came in handy when one was putting off some
task that had to be done. For a shove in the right direction all
we needed was—"Lazarus, get up out of that!"

Another favorite of ours was from the story of a cowboy
who had taken his mail-order bride to his remote ranch. Eventually he came to town for supplies. When he was asked about
his wife he said, "Waal, she got her foot caught in a gopher
hole and broke her leg and I had to shoot the pore li'l thing."
When either of us was feeling particularly down we would
say, "I guess you'll have to shoot the pore li'l thing."

In May Howard thought it would be a lovely idea if we
went to London for the opening of *The Sound of Music*. I
thought so too. Russel and Anna Crouse were going and so
were Dick and Dorothy Rodgers. We anticipated a gay time
with all of us together.

One of the things I always looked forward to in England
was a trip to Brighton, only one hour by train, to see again the
fantastic Royal Pavilion built in 1783 for the Prince of Wales
who would one day be King George IV—and to go shopping
in the narrow winding lanes that were lined with antique
shops. On the day of the opening I went there with my darling old friend Eileen Maremont who was living in London.
We both love the Pavilion and we are both antique hounds, so
we went Pavilion looking and antique shopping. Howard had
not wanted to come with us because he had a lunch appointment with one of his old friends. We were living at the
Mayfair. We had sent our evening clothes down to be pressed
because that night was to be a very formal affair. It was a
benefit performance and we were to meet the Duchess of
Kent there.

In Brighton Eileen and I had lunch and took a three-o'clock train back to London. I got to the hotel about four and was surprised to find Howard in bed with a hot-water bottle at his feet and two quilts over him. He said he felt too hot so I removed the quilts and opened a window. Then I found the thermometer and took his temperature. It read: 106! Of course there was something wrong with the thermometer. So I shook it down and tried again. It still read 106. My heart stood still. I rushed to the other room and closed the door. I phoned to my dear friend Fleur and screamed to her in a whisper that Howard was terribly sick and that she must somehow get a doctor for us right away. She called her doctor and told him that it didn't matter how many patients he had waiting he must get to the Mayfair at once. Luckily his office was in the vicinity and he arrived in about twenty minutes. In the meanwhile I had sent for ice and put a cold cloth on Howard's head and a lump of ice in his mouth. Just then the valet brought in my evening dress. I tried to hang up the damn dress, which was difficult as the wardrobe facilities in this hotel must have been designed for the tall men of the Black Watch. The hooks seemed about eight feet from the floor. I kept putting more cold cloths on Howard's head and ice in his mouth while I tried to get enough bedclothes and underthings off the floor to make a path for the doctor. He came and after making a quick examination he told me quietly that Howard should be put in the hospital at once. I said, "For God's sake, *yes*—and as soon as possible!" The doctor made a couple of phone calls and told me there would be a room ready for him in one hour at the London Clinic and that the ambulance would pick him up. I packed what things I thought Howard might need and also my own nightgown and toothbrush—between more cold cloths and more ice. I tried to call Buck to tell him to cancel our seats, but the Crouses were not in. The ambulance finally arrived after I had called the doctor's office to find out where it was. That ambulance ride is something to be remembered—no nonsense about box springs and foam-rubber mattresses. They wrapped him in blankets and took him out in something that looked like a beach chair. The ambulance was a sort of glorified station wagon with long and rather narrow benches—

I guess you would call them beds—on either side. They were of hard leather, and there was a hard leather pillow for his head. I knelt on the floor and held him to keep him from slipping off. I tried to make a joke and poor Howard said, "Don't make me laugh. It hurts too much." That blessed Fleur and her blessed husband, Tom, in full evening dress (they had evidently broken some engagement) were waiting for us at the entrance of the hospital. Never in my life have I been so glad to see anyone. They stayed at the hospital until midnight and then went to the Claridge to see Buck and Anna when they got back from the theatre and tell them what had happened. The doctor, his name was Cecil Epple, was simply wonderful. He did exactly all the right things. He also called in a lung specialist for consultation. That doctor arrived about midnight. Dr. Epple got a place for me to sleep—a little room in which I did no sleeping that night. It was pneumonia and pleurisy and I hoped Howard would never learn how close to death he was. At five in the morning his fever had gone down two degrees, and by seven, two more degrees. And I began to breathe again and to feel a flooding of indescribable gratitude, first to God, then to the doctors, and then to Fleur.

Three days later his temperature was normal. That was the day the doctors—there were three of them—asked me to meet with them in the little wicker-furnished and chintz-curtained waiting room. They told me that it had been discovered that Howard had leukemia and did I know what that meant? I managed to choke out that I thought it was cancer of the blood. They told me it was, and that there was no known cure for the disease, but that people sometimes had regressions which meant that the patients could have periods when they were apparently well and that those periods sometimes lasted a long time. I told the doctors that Howard must never find out that he had leukemia. He must never be robbed of hope.

I pulled myself together and went back to his room with the terrible secret heavy on my heart. It came to me somehow as a surprise to see him looking so well.

We had been told that London Clinic was the best hospital in the city and Howard actually looked better than he had before he got sick. He was so fond of his doctors and his nurses that he said flippantly, "In the future I plan always to come to London to be sick." The nurses, who were mostly young and mostly Irish, were all impressed with his flowers—"The best since Elizabeth Taylor was here." Buck, who was never to know what I knew, wanted to cancel the booking for his trip home but I wouldn't let him because I knew it would worry Howard, and Buck must never suspect the awful truth. But I kept in close touch with him by phone every day. Howard got well. I read to him a lot during his convalescence and we always looked forward to the tea hour with little sandwiches and cakes and delicious tea. It was our favorite meal. Sometimes our friends had food sent in from good restaurants. Many people came to see him—Emily Kimbrough, who happened to be in London, came to call, bringing with her Madame Pandit, that charming lady who was the ambassador from India and the sister of Prime Minister Nehru. When Howard was well enough to travel we booked passage on the *Queen Mary*. We sailed on June twenty-first, my birthday, and what a wonderful birthday present that was.

Howard had a regression that lasted nearly two years, with only an occasional sick day. I lied to everyone—told them that since his pneumonia he had been left with a chronic bronchitis. I was afraid that if anyone knew, Howard might somehow suspect. No one but the doctors and I must ever know. Dr. Eli Bauman, that saint of a man who had been our doctor for so many years, kept in close touch with us. When Howard seemed ill or ran a temperature even if it was three in the morning, I never hesitated to call the doctor and he never hesitated to come.

The second summer Howard was so well that with the doctor's approval we took a trip to Switzerland, where we had never been before. We stayed in an elegant old-world sort of hotel in the town of Vevey. Our room was comfortable. It had a little balcony that looked out over Lake Geneva where the small passenger boats tootled back and forth like streetcars. On clear days we could see the opposite shore, which was France. Sometimes we would get aboard any boat that came along and sit in deck chairs in the sun, and admire the Alps and the water and the swans, and the charming old villages with their flower-decked wharves where the boat stopped. We would sometimes get off at an attractive place and wait for the next boat to take us back. Howard actually got a tan for the first time in his life and looked the picture of health. On fine days we would often hire a car with an English-speaking driver and drive high into the Alps to spend an afternoon in Gruyere or Gstaad. We would have dinner in some little flower box of an inn and then drive back by dark.

Those were the days when I would try to fool myself into thinking that the doctors had been wrong.

Gruyere is a beautiful medieval village topped with a fairy-tale castle. We loved it. One stands on the castle ramparts and looks down an unbelievable distance below at red-roofed towns and tiny chalets clinging to the sides of mountains, and at the private airfield so far below that the yellow planes landing there looked like the smallest of toys. We were so entranced with it all that we drove back the next day and then drove on to Gstaad where we had cocktails and dinner at a lovely small inn and then drove back at night. We were so very happy.

We had dinner one night with Noël Coward in his beautiful chalet high, high in the mountains above Montreux. His powder room was papered entirely with the sheet-music covers of the songs he had written. Before dinner I told him that my favorite of all his songs was "Where Are the Songs We Sung?" He responded with his usual grace that it was one of his favorites too. He said that after dinner he would play and sing everything I asked for. He did just that. The whole evening was magic and I shall never forget it. The song was:

> Where are the songs we sung
> When love in our hearts was young,
> Where in the limbo of the swiftly passing years
> Lie all our dreams and hopes and tears?
> Where are they now?
> Words that rang so true
> When love in our hearts was new
> Where in the shadows that we have to pass among,
> Lie the songs that once we sung?

Noël Coward has been my hero ever since I first saw him in *Private Lives* many years ago. The day he came to see us in *Life With Father* was disaster for me, and he displayed what seems to me the ultimate in tact and kindness. Knowing he was out front I was so eager to give a good performance that I was very nervous. In the first breakfast table scene I choked on a piece of toast. It went down my windpipe instead of my throat. I could hardly speak and I played the rest of the performance in something slightly above a whisper. When he came backstage afterward, he was much too wise to tell me I had been good, which he knew I would recognize as a lie. Instead he simply popped into the dressing room, gave me a kiss, and said, "I suppose you think you spoiled the whole performance. Well, you didn't."

The night before we left for home we wanted to make it some particular kind of celebration to culminate a wonderful summer. We decided to get on one of the boats—they all had restaurants—have our dinner and get off at some village and come back on another boat whenever we felt like it. We got aboard and went immediately to its restaurant. Then we learned that this particular boat was not making its trip down the lake as usual, but was going straight across to France. Naturally, we didn't have our passports with us, so we were put off at a deserted pier, still in Switzerland, and had to wait there until the boat returned to take us back. We were hysterical with laughter by that time. It was raining. I had my camera with me and we took flashlight pictures of each other standing on the deserted pier with the dim lights of Vevey on one side and the dim lights of the French port on the other.

The next day we sailed for home on our favorite ship, the *Queen Mary*. We had crossed on it so many times before.

The following winter Howard was up and dressed most of the time. He even made an occasional visit to his beloved Players Club. When it was summer we decided to go to the farm for my birthday and stay there for some time. We went on a perfect midsummer day and I was so happy to see the farm again after a long absence. Howard sat on the porch while I ran beside the brook with open arms down to the woods. When I came back Howard said he was not feeling well. I put him to bed and took his temperature. It was high enough to be alarming. I didn't want to frighten him, and I could not make any phone calls as the only phone was in our bedroom, so I made the excuse I was driving to the nearest town, which was Flemington, to get some magazines. Instead, I drove to the only neighbor we knew and asked her where I could get a doctor. She gave me the name and phone number of her doctor in a nearby town. Three hours later he came and recommended that Howard be put in the Hunterdon County Medical Center Hospital, which was only three miles away. We got an ambulance about midnight. I followed with the car. I stayed with him until three o'clock in the morning when his temperature had gone down a little, and then drove back to the farm. It was pneumonia again.

My dear friends Gladys and Charles, when they heard the news, drove down to the country to be with me. I hardly saw them except for an occasional meal or when I drove back from the hospital at night, but it was a comfort to have them there.

Howard stayed in that very good hospital about four weeks. In the meanwhile the doctors had discovered he needed surgery. After the pneumonia was over and he had gotten some strength back, we drove him from one hospital straight to another. This was St. Luke's in New York, where a very fine surgeon whom I knew was on the staff. The surgery was successful. Howard stayed in the hospital three weeks.

While he was in there I had his bedroom all done over for his return. The walls were painted a sunny yellow, a new yellow candlewick bed cover, and red geraniums on his mantel underneath his favorite picture. The picture shows a scene near Gloucester. It is of a house with people playing croquet on the lawn, and a little gazebo built high on the top of a huge boulder and reached by a small wooden stairway.

The next year, the day before Thanksgiving, we went to St. Luke's by ambulance. It was pneumonia again, but he was not as frighteningly ill as he had been before. The first thing I always did when he entered a hospital was to warn the doctors and the head nurse and to tell her to warn the other nurses that Howard was not to know the real nature of his illness. There was only a very small room available for him, just space enough for a bed and one chair. We had our Thanksgiving dinner together off our trays. St. Luke's is in Harlem and this was when the race riots there were at their height. I stayed until ten o'clock, not knowing that the hospital closed at nine. The front was all locked and dark. I found my way through a labyrinth of corridors to a back entrance. There was a long dark block to Morningside Drive. The attendant said, "If you see a man, or particularly if you see two men coming toward you, turn right around and come back to the hospital. Don't walk. Run." I managed the dark block and fortunately God was good to me and I got a taxi.

In trying to fight his third bout with pneumonia the doctors in desperation had given him a new medicine. He reacted badly to it. His fever shot up so high that they had to pack his poor body in ice. He was delirious for three days. I saw tears in Dr. Bauman's eyes for he loved Howard. I sat at the foot of his bed and heard him talk intermittently about the theatre in his delirium. "Is the curtain up? Why doesn't the curtain go up?" The crisis passed and he started to get better. I had him moved to a big corner room with windows on two sides. I brought his favorite picture and had it hung and lighted so that he could go to sleep with all the other lights turned off and only the light on the peaceful scene in the picture. He liked going to sleep that way. By Christmastime he had gained back some strength. He was sitting up in bed and making jokes. In the hospital Christmas was everywhere—windows painted with holiday scenes and carols played on patients' radios. I decorated Howard's room and brought up a small tree with lights. We learned that Bill Blass, the famous designer of clothes, was in the hospital two doors down the hall. He was ambulatory so we invited him in for a Christmas Eve cocktail. The three of us drank bourbon out of those hospital glasses filled with that hospital shaved ice. We lighted the tree and opened a few presents that were easy to handle. It was all very pleasant and cheerful because Howard was better.

He came home. He loved his "new room." He used to say, "If you have to be sick, this is the way to do it." A huge tree, as tall as our house, grew in the back and pressed its fernlike leaves against Howard's windows and against mine in the room above. It was an ailanthus, that valiant city tree that holds its own against poor soil, polluted air, and cement sidewalks. He got better in the summer. Sometimes he would walk around the block with me, with occasional stops to rest. There was an intercom buzzer between his room and mine. On particularly bad nights he would call my room at two or three or four in the morning. I would go down. We would talk a little and then I would lie down beside him with my arms around him until he went to sleep. I was overwhelmingly grateful to be needed.

In October the City Center Theatre did a revival of *Life With Father* for a run of three weeks. I was asked to play my original part, and Howard particularly urged me to. I was finally convinced that I was not too old. We all thought that having the play done again would give Howard a lift. The night before it opened the flu hit me with a sledgehammer blow. I played the first week and then my voice gave out and I had to go to bed for three days while my understudy played. Leon Ames was in Howard's part. I finished the three-week run. The play was warmly received, but I was glad when it was over. The hardest part of it had been that I dared not go near Howard during that time for fear he would catch the flu from me. And the saddest part of it all was that Howard had not been able to see any of it, not even a rehearsal. While I had the flu we talked on the intercom, which was better than nothing.

Our little Siamese cat, Madam, made her home on Howard's bed and he loved having her there. She used to stand with her hind paws on his bed and her front paws on the bed table and drink out of his water glass. This pleased Howard enormously. He would sometimes say, "Dorothy, fill the glass up to the top so she can reach it more easily." Frank Loesser, the composer who wrote the music for *Guys and Dolls* and so many other great songs, used to come to see Howard. One day he saw Madam's performance. The next day he sent Howard a beautiful little crystal pitcher with a wide opening at the top for Madam's convenience.

Ann McPhillips came into our lives making them richer. She was a fine nurse and an adorable person. She was young and pretty and very Irish. Her speech, while not really a brogue, nevertheless had a little lilt to it. She was cheerful and funny and very good at her job. I would hear her singing when she came to work in the mornings. She stayed all day and sometimes into the evening. We both loved her dearly and she was soon devoted to Howard. He had a color-TV set at the foot of his bed with a remote-control switch. He loved watching all sports. It didn't matter which kind. It could be baseball, football, basketball, or tennis. I had never had any interest in sports so it was wonderful to find that Ann was a sports fan and could share the enthusiasm with Howard. She would pull up a chair beside his bed and they both felt that they had a good seat in the bleachers. Ann, without knowing she was doing it, helped to lighten the burden on my heart.

I played a part in a television show after having gotten a night nurse for Howard so that he would never be alone. It was a one-hour show and money was lavished on it. Tony Perkins was starred and I, playing a ninety-year-old zombie, was featured. It was called *Evening Primrose* and was a dramatization of a horror fantasy written by John Collier. The show was difficult technically and required a lot of rehearsing. One day we worked from early morning until ten o'clock at night. I got home completely exhausted and discovered I had lost my key. I rang the doorbell and the nurse let me in. I kissed Howard good night, pulled my dress off and was ready to fall into bed when I realized that I would have to wake the cook to tell her I had a six-o'clock call the next morning. I went up to the fourth floor and couldn't wake her by knocking, so I opened the door a few inches and noticed there was an odd light in the room. My first thought was that she had gone to sleep with her TV set on and the sound turned down. I had barely time to register the fact that there were four lighted candles in a pan on the floor when the bedclothes caught fire. I shoved her out the door and pulled the mattress over the candles and the burning bedclothes to try to smother the flames. Then I ran for the fire extinguisher in the closet. I didn't know how to work the thing so I pushed and pulled everything until something went off. I handed it to the cook and then started running for all the other fire extinguishers in the house—in the meantime yelling to Howard to call the Fire Department and to the nurse to open the front doors so the firemen could get in. The most terrifying part of it was not the flames but the smoke. It was possible to stay in the room only as long as I could hold my breath, then I had to run out and gulp some air before I could go back in. The firemen came in about fifteen minutes and finished off the remaining sparks. All that was left of the bed was the charred frame and the springs. Thank God, the smoke had not gotten down as far as Howard's floor.

Of course the cook would not admit it, but she must have been doing voodoo rites. The candles were in a square pan, one in each corner. I have been told that means north, south, east, and west, and is one of the fundamentals of voodoo.

The next winter the doctors thought that Howard should be in a warmer climate so we went to Palm Beach for the worst part of the winter. It did no good. He was in bed most of the time. I had an oxygen tank put next to his bed and I read to him a lot. Before leaving New York we had made our train reservations to return there on April third. We were all packed and dressed and waiting for a call telling us the car was ready to take us to the station. The phone rang. It was Peggy calling us from New York to tell us that Buck had died. We tried to get seats on a plane, but because of a railroad strike in Florida and a great cutback in train service there was no space for us on any plane.

We got in the car shocked and numb. When we arrived at the station we found that the train would be four hours late. I telephoned Anna from a phone booth to tell her we were not able to get space on a plane and that our train would be very late. Buck and Anna had been in Puerto Rico for their daughter's spring vacation, and we had talked to them there only a few days ago. We did not know that Buck had suddenly developed pneumonia and that they had flown him back to put him in St. Luke's Hospital.

When we got to Washington, Howard got off the train to phone the *Times* about some mistake that had been made in Buck's obituary. It was very cold there. I followed him out with his overcoat and hat and bundled him up while we waited interminably for the phone booth to be free. Our train finally got to New York nine hours late. There was a wheelchair waiting for Howard.

On May 27 there was a memorial service for Buck held by the Dramatists Guild at the Broadhurst Theatre. There were beautiful tributes to him. Poor Howard was not able to go, so I went to represent him as well as myself. I told the people in the audience that Howard was too ill to be present and that he had tried to compose a message, but his feeling for Buck went far beyond anything he was able to put into words—just yet. He tried and tried and he thought that anything he attempted to say seemed trite and inadequate. He finally broke down and said, "I can't do it. Buck isn't here to help me."

I read Russel's favorite passage from the Bible—the fourteenth chapter of the Gospel according to John. It begins: "Let not your heart be troubled,"—it ends with, "Peace I leave with you, my peace I give unto you, not as the world giveth, give I unto you. Let not your heart be troubled, neither let it be afraid."

John Mason Brown said in part: "To the world Buck is Russel Crouse who with Howard Lindsay became Lindsay and Crouse, with the two names so eliding, one into the other, that we think of them as one name. More than being a fusion ticket, they were two theatre men whose typewriters beat as one. They practiced the vanishing art of the well-made play. There was nothing sick about them and nothing angry and nothing beat. They relished nonsense. They knew the values of a plot. They loved the music which is laughter. They never suffered from self-pity. As a team they had vast hopes and no pretensions. Huge success and no conceit. I admired Buck as a man and I loved him as a friend. His modesty was as all conquering as his kindness. When Buck died he took a piece of me with him."

Howard was getting thinner and weaker all the time. It was breaking my heart to see him gradually disappear. It would have been a little easier if I could have talked about it to someone, but of course I couldn't because the secret must be kept. Howard must never be robbed of hope. I have just found a page that had been torn out of my diary and hidden. It has no date. It was written in the small hours because I had no one to talk to but myself. It said: "I need someone to talk to now —right now. I need Howard, that's who, but I can't talk with him because he is dying, and he must never ever know it, nor must anyone else know it. I am afraid that even the thought of it in someone else's mind somehow might get through to him. Everyone must think he is going to get well. He must believe it. But I have stopped talking to him about how much better he looks and about all the things we will do when he gets well. The disappointment for him is too great when he has setbacks. For a man who used to be something of a hypochondriac, he is remarkably innocent about diseases. My heart turns over when I see an article about leukemia in some magazine that we both read. Of course I must never try to hide it. But if he reads the piece it apparently makes no impression on him. The doctors and I are the only ones who know."

Howard never complained. The most I ever heard him say was, "I am awfully tired of being sick." He sometimes said, "I love this room with the tree coming in the window," and "Aren't we lucky to have this house?" He had visitors quite often. Brooks Atkinson, the drama critic on the *Times*, came frequently. John Lindsay, the mayor, came to see him too. I read to him a lot, continuing our habit of sharing books.

One day when I hurt too much I went to a minister whom I had met only once to see if he could say anything that would bolster my courage or ease my spirit, but he was of no help. These were the times when I had to remind myself that all I had to do was to say the next line. Howard was not suffering physical pain, he was simply fading away. That Christmas he was a little better, well enough to come down to the living room in pajamas and robe and watch me trim the tree. Once in a while when the nurse was with Howard, or when he was watching a game on TV, or when he was asleep, I would go out and walk, or sometimes get on a bus and ride to wherever it was going. When I was particularly heartsick I would go down to the kitchen where our little cat Madam slept at night. She always welcomed me with open paws. As soon as I sat down she would jump in my lap and start her loud purring. It was one of the things to do—a comforting thing.

The next Christmas he was not well enough to be up at all, so I brought the small tree to his bedroom, and we had our Christmas Eve dinner together there. Our next-door neighbors are an order of nuns who knew that Howard was ill. They asked if they might come and sing some Christmas carols for him, so they came to our living room and sang their carols. Howard listened from his room above and I from the top step of the stairway.

In February a terrible thing happened. He got shingles. The skin specialist told me afterward that we were lucky because many people suffered great pain with them. Howard had no pain, only discomfort. All he said was "Well, thank God, I've got something at last that the doctors have a name for!" So I learned for certain that he had never known he had leukemia. One night in February I kissed Howard good night, and as we had just finished reading *Nicholas and Alexandra* that day, we agreed we would start the new book tomorrow. At about three in the morning the night nurse called me. He was in terrible pain. I called the doctor. He came and gave Howard an injection that stopped the pain. That afternoon I was sitting beside him holding his hand under the covers. He knew he was surrounded by love. He turned his head and looked at me with perfectly clear and bright eyes and said, "I'm not going to get well. It's been a wonderful journey with a wonderful companion, and I've enjoyed every foot of the way." Ten minutes later he was dead.

With the inestimable help of Anna Crouse I devised a memorial service a few days after Howard's death because I knew so many people would want the opportunity to say some sort of good-bye. The service was held in the large Madison Avenue Presbyterian Church. I have been told that six hundred people were there. I wanted so much to do it in a way that I thought Howard would have approved. I selected and edited the psalms, and the minister spoke them simply and clearly and with conviction. I asked four men to speak—Sidney Kingsley, the playwright, to speak for the Dramatists Guild and the Authors League of America; Alexander Lindey, the lawyer, for the Dramatists Play Service; Paddy Chayefsky, the playwright, for the New Dramatists, and Dennis King, the actor, for The Players.

Here is a very small part of what Sidney Kingsley said: ". . . our deep gratitude and affection for this good man . . . As a dramatist he found one of those collaborations that are made in heaven. He found our equally good and beautiful Russel Crouse. Together they created some of the most telling and successful plays of our time. Together they won the Pulitzer Prize. Together they became a theatre legend. There was a letter from Mayor John Lindsay to Dorothy which said, 'We are thinking of you and praying for you. The memory of Howard will be with us always, and with New York and with the country.' And it will be, largely because Howard was a yeasayer. He practiced and taught the affirmation of Life. The job Howard derived and communicated through all his activities finally characterizes him as a complete, fulfilled good man."

Alexander Lindey said among a great many other things: "Long after our eulogies are forgotten Howard will be remembered for his creative achievements in the theatre and for the tradition of public service he honored. These will be his memorial."

Here is a very small part of Paddy Chayefsky's speech: "He gave the New Dramatists many things—his time, his energy, his money, his theatre. But more than anything he gave those qualities that celebrated him as a man, his substance, his self-respect and his integrity. I shall miss him and his indestructible decency more than I am willing to admit right now."

Dennis King, who succeeded Howard as president of The

Players, started his speech with a poem written for The
Players by Don Marquis:

> "I have seen ghosts of men I never knew
> Great, gracious souls, the golden hearts of earth
> Look from the shadows of those rooms we love
> Living a wistful instance in our mirth
> I have seen Jefferson smile down at Drew,
> And Booth pause musing on the stair above.

"And now we of The Players will always see Howard mus-
ing on the stair above. His official deeds are glowing and a
matter of record. What many people do not know, and as
Howard would wish it, never know, are the countless acts of
kindness and generosity he performed for his Fellow Players."

The Players Club was closed during the time of the service.
Their quarterly bulletin was devoted entirely to Howard. The
first page was blank except for a quote from Shakespeare:

> Farewell, worthy lord,
> A heavy heart bears not a nimble tongue.

For the service there had been cards printed with one verse
and the chorus of "The Battle Hymn of the Republic," which
was our favorite hymn. As I had hoped, the whole congrega-
tion—or should I say audience—joined with the choir in singing it. They sang it loud and strong and the service ended with
a glory hallelujah.

> "He has sounded out the trumpet that shall never
> call retreat,
> He is sifting out the hearts of men before his
> judgment seat,
> Oh be swift my soul to answer Him
> Be jubilant my feet,"

I am sure that Howard's soul was swift and that his feet were
jubilant.

February 15, 1968

Dear Mrs. Lindsay:

I've been talking to my wife about the memorial service
today and how deeply impressive it was. I have to tell you

before I go to sleep that few things in this battered old world have struck me with having so much dignity, honesty, and love as this hour for Howard. Moments like this in one's life stand apart. They make the whole life process mean something fine. A stranger walking into that church today would have found himself touched to the best part of himself by the evoking of what is best in all of us.

I cannot get over the power of emotion that was there, and the dignity and restraint which held it in focus. I left the church feeling better—feeling that the good instincts we sometimes want to banish are the toughest and the best. It made me proud to be alive.

                                        Yours,
                                        Hal Holbrook

The letters poured in that he was a good man, a good citizen and a kind person, and that innumerable people loved him and admired him. All that gave me great pride, of course, but what gave me great comfort were the things that only a few knew—the smile that always answered mine, the special tenderness, the admirations and the indignations that we shared, the songs we sung and the books we read, and the laughs we had together. These had been the worst and the best years of my life—for even with the underlying pain I had sometimes been overtaken unexpectedly by moments of joy that astonished my heart. Howard gave me the greatest gift any man could give to the woman who loves him—he needed me.

I wrote to Fleur not to worry about me—that I could cope, but I wasn't as sure as I sounded. It was hell. Worse than I dreamed it could be. Even with all the help of my wonderful friends and even with all the years I had had to prepare for this. I learned that nothing really prepares one for desolation, that heartache is not a figure of speech but an actual physical pain.

I knew all the things I had to be grateful for and I listed them often in my mind. I was overwhelmingly grateful to Fleur. I felt that she had given me the last seven years of Howard's life, for I believe he surely would have died in London if she had not been there when I reached out for help. These last years had been good ones in many ways in spite of the burden of the knowledge of his leukemia that was always with me. The house had never seemed large before—now it was enormous. I told myself that I would get used to it. Howard's adorable little nurse stayed with me for the first few nights. I knew that I must soon start looking for a live-in cook or couple, and I thanked God for our beautiful Peggy, not only because she knew everything about our affairs but because of her being a special and wonderful human being; and I had always loved her very much.

In December Howard and I had been told that we were jointly to receive the March of Dimes Award on the eleventh of May. This charity was begun during Franklin Roosevelt's presidency and was used to finance research on polio. It is also known as the Mary MacArthur Memorial Award. Helen Hayes's daughter, Mary MacArthur, had died at the age of eighteen of polio and this was also to commemorate her. Since then, thanks to the Salk vaccine, polio has almost disappeared. The fund is now used for research on birth defects in children. Howard died in February so I had to accept the citation for both of us in May. Mayor John Lindsay spoke and Helen Hayes made the presentation, which was graceful and flattering. The dinner was beautifully done and I might have enjoyed it if I could have made the acceptance speech at the beginning of the evening instead of waiting till the end. They used slides of Howard and me thrown on a large screen from photographs of us dating from the year one. It was accompanied by a running commentary by David Wayne and Cornelia Otis Skinner standing on either side of the stage. To end the affair there were three songs from three of Howard and Buck's shows. It was the only thing of its kind I had ever been to that was not too long.

I went to North Dakota to get an honorary degree from Dickinson State College which made me a Doctor of Fine Arts. So if I were ever to see any fine arts that needed doctoring I would be on hand to make house calls.

Going to North Dakota was like stepping into a different

world, and I was in the frame of mind where I could use a different one. I asked the president of the college about student rebellions. He said, "We never heard of them. The kids here really want to get an education."

When last I saw the college it had been fifty years before. It consisted of one stark building standing on a rise of ground in the middle of the prairie. Now I found there were at least twelve beautiful buildings, a handsomely landscaped campus, a well-equipped theatre, wonderful athletic facilities, and students who liked being there. The whole thing was very gratifying and deeply touching. There were huge signs that said "Welcome Home, Dorothy Stickney." A bank even had one of those running electric signs, the kind they have on the Times Building. I had no ties there as the one remaining member of my family—my sister—had died ten years earlier. But it was good to see my few old friends. The hotel was directly across the street from the railroad station and I could hear the lovely sound of trains, the sound I used to listen to as a child, the sound that held such promise for me. I kept saying to myself, "It's wonderful to be here, but only for a little while," and the trains kept reminding me that I would soon be on my way.

I went to the farm in New Jersey twice, but found that I missed Howard unbearably there, much worse than at the house in town. Perhaps the combination of beauty and loneliness is too much for any heart to take.

I found myself rather surprised when the summer was over and had been gotten through. I weekended away from town occasionally, but most of the time I stayed at home in my airconditioned house, or I was kept very busy due to my loving friends, and also trying to get the house in shape after such long neglect. I had let things get terribly shabby through the years of Howard's illness as the only two rooms that held any interest for me were his bedroom and mine. There were so many hours of happiness as well as agony when I was with him in his room, and so many hours when I was alone in mine praying and trying to get ready for what must come. I found the house a great comfort in a curious way; even without

Howard it gave me a feeling of shelter and protection. I no longer belonged to a person but I did belong to a place. Some of my friends thought I was crazy to live in this big house instead of a small apartment, but I decided to keep right on being crazy. Howard and I had lived here for twenty years and we loved the place. We often used to say when we closed the door behind us, "Aren't we lucky to have this house?"

I redid the curtains, bought new lampshades, and finally accomplished a week-long job of cleaning the library and sorting the books. It had not been done for five years. I gave away vast quantities of books trying to make room on the shelves, but after I had finished they seemed to look as full as ever. I gave a few performances of *A Lovely Light* that winter, and I did a couple of TV shows, but nothing in the theatre, and I found I didn't care a bit. My little Siamese cat, Madam, had died just two weeks after Howard did. That was a low blow. I still think it was her own decision. She simply didn't eat anything except what she could lick off my fingers and of course that wasn't enough.

I really believed I was doing pretty well at this point. The heartache was no longer continuous. There had been times of feeling actually happy—and then of course there had been the moments when I would bump into the blank wall of Howard's absence with the same old feeling of shock and incredulity. To borrow the words from one of Edna St. Vincent Millay's letters: "We had a grand time, but it's a changed world. The presence of that absence is everywhere." Nevertheless, I knew that I was better and that gave me great encouragement.

Peggy and I finally finished replying to the hundreds of letters of condolence. It took us nearly a year. I got through the holidays well enough considering it was the first Christmas I had spent away from Howard in forty-one years. We had started trimming the tree and unwrapping the presents together two years before we were married. I had carefully built up my defenses against the first Christmas Eve—dinner in a restaurant with friends and then the theatre. But the best-laid plans of mice and men—et cetera—I got a recurrence of the flu and spent Christmas Eve in bed with a slight fever and reading a novel about the South Seas. Nevertheless, I was on my feet again Christmas Day, having the same open-house party that Howard and I had had for so many years—surrounded by friends and with a few strangers thrown in for good measure.

I went to London the next summer. My friend Eileen had sublet a charming little flat for me at 15 Grosvenor Square, just half a block down from the American embassy. It was bright colored and cheerful, and the little kitchen was just right for getting my breakfast and tea, and Eileen and I did a lot of antique shopping together.

While I was away a real estate agent had rented the farmhouse to less than ideal tenants. They had six children, two cats and a dog that was in the puppy stage of chewing things up. I couldn't get rid of them until their year's lease was up.

When I came home early in autumn I went into Brian Friel's play called *The Mundy Scheme*. We had previews for two weeks before the opening, and we closed three days later.

Peggy and I went to Palm Beach in February. I wanted to be away from home during that month. We had a good two weeks with complete cooperation from the weather. We soaked up sun and clean air, we shopped on Worth Avenue, and read novels and went to bed early.

I gave a performance of *A Lovely Light* on the way back. It felt good to be working again, and surprisingly enough there was little strain connected with it.

On the night before Thanksgiving I went alone to see the film *Camelot*. When I came home I locked the door and got as far as the lowest step of the stairs when the dam burst. I sat there and howled and yelled. There was no one in the house to hear me so I let go. My cat, whom I had acquired after Madam died, came down the stairs and sat on my lap and licked my face. Maybe it was salt, or maybe from the noise I had been making the cat thought it was another animal. Anyway, that's what happened and perhaps it was just as well to get it over with. It was time to remind myself that all I had to do was to say the next line. It could make the impossible possible—a line at a time and I could cope.

I began to feel better physically and I started emerging from the fog of indifference that I had been walking around in for so many months. Life once more had started to be interesting. I was getting things done to spruce up the house. I was even beginning once more to read the theatre section of the Sunday *Times*. I went to Richmond and gave a performance of *A Lovely Light*. The college people were a splendid audience and the play went well.

The following summer I went to London again for a few weeks and took Peggy with me. When we came home life seemed to have turned a corner and I could think of Howard without such a pang. Happiness came my way sometimes and was always a lovely surprise. I had no plans, just went along putting one day after another and welcoming any unexpected treasures that came my way.

Early in the summer I had made a recording of *A Lovely Light*. It is an album of two long-playing records. It turned out very well and I was proud of it.

Of course the first thing I had done after getting back from London was to go to the farm and view the holocaust. The walls were still standing, but the inside was pretty much of a shambles. My darling house. I got to work immediately getting things repaired and replaced.

I went back into the theatre and stayed for over a year in 1973 and 1974. No one in the world was more surprised than I. One day my agent called and asked if I would like to play the grandmother in the rock musical *Pippin*. I said, "What on earth made you think of me? I have never been in a musical in my life, and I don't sing or dance." He told me that since the death of Irene Ryan, who had played the part originally, they had not been able to find the right person for the role. Irene Ryan had been a TV personality when she played Granny in a series called "The Beverly Hillbillies." She had opened in *Pippin* in the fall and had played it until March when she got sick and had to leave. She went back to her home in California and died there. The agent asked me if I would mind auditioning for the part. I said, "Mind? I wouldn't do it any other way. The sooner they find out my limitations, the better it will be."

The audition was set for the following week. This was really a challenge to be met. I knew there was not the remotest chance of my getting the part, but I did not want my audition to be an embarrassment for me nor for the people sitting out front, who would be the producer, Stuart Ostrow, and the director, Robert Fosse. So, knowing how embarrassing auditions can be I got a man from the orchestra in the *Irene* company to come and teach me the song, as I cannot read music. We worked on it for that week until I learned it. The day of the audition came and I was only mildly nervous because I was so sure that after they had heard me that would be the end of it.

Lo and behold—two days later they called and offered me the part at a very good salary. The part was Berthe who was the mother of Charlemagne and the grandmother of Pippin. She had a scene with Pippin, played by John Rubinstein, and a good song with clever lyrics. The scene was really a little fifteen-minute vaudeville act, and a very good one. I wore a white wig and a wonderfully pretty costume. Pippin has come to his grandmother for advice, and she sings to him:

> "When you are as old as I, my dear,
> And I hope that you never are,
> You will woefully wonder why, my dear,
> Through your cataracts and catarrh
> You could squander away or sequester
> A drop of a precious year.
> For when your best days are yester,
> The rest-er twice as dear."

I rehearsed with only the stage manager and the resident pianist. I never saw or heard the orchestra until one hour before the curtain went up on my opening night. The chorus boys and girls, whom I was beginning to know, were all rooting for me. They dressed in the basement, but they came upstairs to listen and silently applaud when I finished. Apparently I had gotten away with it all right.

After two verses and two choruses a curtain made to look like a roll of parchment came down at the back of the stage with the words and music of the chorus on it. It even had the little bouncing-ball effect, the kind that was used to indicate the words when popular songs were thrown on the screen in the old-time movie houses. This was the chorus:

> Oh it's time to start livin'
> Time to take a little
> From the world we're given
> Time to take time
> For Spring will turn to Fall
> In just no time at all.

On the third time round the audience joined in singing and clapping in rhythm. I never got over being surprised at finding myself in a rock musical belting out a rock song with five chorus boys back of me and an orchestra in front of me. But I loved going on the stage and hated coming back to my dressing room. There was always much applause when we made the exit with the five boys carrying me offstage. I left *Pippin* after a year and a month to have a cataract operation on my eye.

When I recovered I went to California to do a Christmas play for television called *The Homecoming*. I played a very innocent old lady bootlegger. We went to a wonderful place called Jackson Hole, in Wyoming, where there was plenty of snow for the location shots. It was fun riding in a sleigh with jingling bells. This was the TV performance that started that very good series called "The Waltons."

I had had my cat, Madam II, for a couple of years and I had just recently acquired a kitten. She was completely enchanting and a great waster of time. She had discovered to my dismay that she could jump as high as a mantel or a chest of drawers, and she got great pleasure out of pushing to the floor any object small enough for her to handle. One winter afternoon she gave me half an hour of sheer joy. It was snowing hard, with big fluffy flakes, and she sat looking out at it—her first snow— through my bedroom window with utter amazement. Every once in a while she would jump up and try to catch a snowflake through the window pane, and during the whole scene she muttered to herself about the wonder of it all.

In May The Players gave a party in my honor and it was a

joyous occasion. I wish Howard had been there. He would have loved it. Shortly after I had done *A Lovely Light* for its Broadway run, I had performed it on television as one of David Susskind's series called "Festival of the Performing Arts." I believe this was the first time that any television performance had been allowed to go for its whole length with no commercial interruptions. The Players had gotten a kinescope of the film of my television performance and showed it on a large screen. I thought it looked much better than I remembered when I saw it on TV back in 1962. The very size seemed to add something special to it. There was a fine buffet supper, and some speeches, and a lot of singing around the piano afterward.

Later that year I had a call from Dickinson State College informing me that the new auditorium was finished and that they wished to name it for me. Of course I was delighted to accept. The Drama Department had been rehearsing to give a performance of *Life With Father* in my honor. I had been in Dickinson for a few days some years before, but this time I was more impressed than ever at all the changes that had taken place. The land on which had once stood our house, the cottonwood trees, our yard, our barn, and our corral was now covered entirely by a shiny Woolworth building. I hope someone was at least a little bit sad at cutting down our big cottonwoods. I stayed at a new inn, one of a chain called Ramada, situated on what is now the outskirts of town. Rocky Butte, where we used to go for picnics, feeling that it was a long distance away from town, is now part of a municipal park. Graveyard Hill, where we used to go coasting in winter, is now a completely built-up suburb called Summit Drive. The prairie, where we used to ride, is now covered with houses all cheek by jowl. I wonder why, with all that prairie space, the houses are built so close together? The ceremony of the naming of the new building was impressive. At the end of my thank-you speech I said:

"We must all have at sometime played that game of 'Who would you like to be if you could be anyone in the world you wanted to be?' Of course the picture changes with the years.

When I was five or six I wanted to be Little Eva in the *Uncle Tom's Cabin* shows that came to town every summer. I used to hang over the fence of our yard open-mouthed with wonder as the little girl in the plumed bonnet riding in a little chariot drawn by Shetland ponies rode by in the parade. When I was older I wanted to go to college and eventually become a teacher. That might have come true except that the trouble with my eyes prevented my getting enough education. I went to drama school instead. And after many bumps and bruises got to be an actress. After I was an actress when I played the game I would wish myself a composer who could write songs that would give people pleasure to sing long after I was dead.

"Do you know what I would rather be than anything in the world right now? I would rather be an auditorium that would house music and dance and drama and lectures and instructions and mass meetings far into the future long after I am gone. Yes, more than anything in the world I would rather be an auditorium."

It was Thanksgiving time—that had been a long time ago— when my house was robbed while I was in the country with friends for the long holiday weekend. I have replaced the stolen silver with plate, and have picked up some costume jewelry. The only thing I still miss vividly is my heart-shaped ring. I sometimes wonder whatever became of the gold locket I wore in *Life With Father*. It was given to me by Mrs. Clarence Day, Jr. It had "Vinnie" engraved on the outside and two pictures of Clare on the inside. Surely this could have been of no value to anyone but me.

It had taken me a long time to straighten up the house from the way the burglars had left it. I wanted to find out from the welter of things that were scattered on the floor and had to be gone through what my life had been about—what was of particular value to me. I found so many things that I can feel my burglars actually did me a favor—so many, *many* things that the burglars *couldn't* take.

Recently I found a verse from the Bible which I had copied

out and stuck in a book so I wouldn't lose it. I have searched my Bible looking for it and simply cannot find it again. Here is just as I wrote it:

> Behold! [What a lovely word that is!]
> Behold! I create new heavens and a new earth;
> And the former things shall not be remembered
>   nor come into mind,
> But be Ye glad and rejoice forever in that which
>   I create;
> For as the days of a tree shall be the days of my
>   people,
> And my chosen shall long enjoy the work of their
>   hands,
> They shall not labor in vain, nor bring forth
>   for calamity.

I am sure that God is creating new heavens and a new earth and that I shall rejoice and be glad in it—and that the former things (at least the bad things) "shall not be remembered nor come into mind." Howard and I certainly had "long enjoyed the work of our hands" and we did not "labor in vain nor bring forth for calamity." Haven't we always been the lucky ones! I love to think of our days as "the days of a tree."

It's extraordinary how certain trees have always played an important part in my life—the cottonwoods in our yard in Dickinson when I was a child—certain trees at the edge of the water in Lakewood—the beautiful rustling poplar tree in our garden when we lived on Eleventh Street—the lovely ailanthus that crowds the windows here at home—and of course my special apple tree in the country that Howard had given me as a present along with the house.

One day in October when I was on the farm a very important thing happened. It had been raining for weeks and the ground was soft and soggy. We had been warned that a hurricane might hit us. But the little house had stood against its hill secure and strong for over two hundred years, and I went to bed unworried. At six in the morning I was awakened by a loud crash. I jumped out of bed and noticed that the room was particularly bright. I looked out the window. My tree was gone. My beautiful special apple tree that had covered one whole side of the house. The first tree that I had ever felt I really owned was lying on the ground with its roots in the air and its heavy weight of apples scattered everywhere. The tail of the hurricane had hit and pushed it over. My beautiful tree that had filled my room with the scent of blossoms in the spring and that had hung red apples in my window at autumn had done its one last kindness—it had not fallen on the house or on the porch, but lay harmlessly across the iris border and the road. It was eventually cut up to make fragrant wood for the two big fireplaces. I shall always miss it, but my room is now full of sunlight, and a wonderful view has opened up that I had never been aware of before. I could now see all the way up to the bend in the road, and that is enough.

INDEX